Inside Houses

Bonner Straße 126, D-50968 Köln

Picture concept by Martin Rosswog
Book based on an original idea by Dr. Andreas Graf

Publishing and Art direction: Peter Feierabend
Project manager: Simone Nörling
Assistance: Monika Schmatz

Layout and typography: Kathrin Jacobsen; Bernd Elfeld, e-design, Bonn

Translation into English: Michael Scuffil
Translation into French: Françoise Ramson, Joëlle Grünastel, Arno Dupin de Beyssat

Carthography: Studio für Landkartentechnik Maiwald, Norderstedt

Reproduction: Fachlabor Lillig/Schirwon, Köln
Lithograhy: Digiprint, Erfurt
Production: Oliver Benecke
Printing and binding: Reálszisztéma Dabasi Nyomda Rt., Dabas
Printed in Hungary

ISBN 3-8290-5914-0
10 9 8 7 6 5 3 2 1

Inside Houses

Rural Homes in Europe
Ländliches Wohnen in Europa / Maisons rustique en Europe

Fotografien und Text von Martin Rosswog

mit einer Einleitung von Andreas Graf

KÖNEMANN

The Art of Inventing and Concealing Art

Photographer Martin Rosswog is a documentary artist. Fired by sociological interest, he collects and preserves, arranges and archives his material, while at the same time his artistic eye reveals people, objects and landscapes in their existential magic. Rosswog displays a farmstead, a bedroom, a village, a kitchen dresser – each, quite literally, in its own light. His camera senses the aura of a form, an object, and makes it radiate from within. He never uses artificial light for his pictures, and dramatic effects based on sunlight are likewise avoided. As a photographer, he makes no attributions, judgments or assessments. As an artist, he remains objective. Not that he does not reveal the esthetic quality of the objects he portrays; on the contrary, he uses the camera to, so to speak, cast light upon them. As a recorder of facts, he is an archivist of passing time, a librarian of the disappearing knowledge of people's circumstances, of the losses due to modernization. He observes, portrays, waits, collects. As an artist, by contrast, he becomes the motor of a transformation. Things do not so much exist, as come into existence by his observation of them. A stove, a cupboard, a vase, a telephone – seen by Rosswog, they unfold a magic life of their own.

Three Major Projects

Martin Rosswog was born in Bergisch Gladbach near Cologne in 1950. For almost twenty years, he has been working on three major interrelated photographic projects, parts of which have already found their way into book form: portraits of people[1], country interiors[2], and exterior views. This order is also more or less chronological. His interest as a photographer has gradually progressed from the individual human being to the human being as a social being; from the fixation of the moment, of what has become (i.e. the portrait), he has gradually moved on to a concern with living conditions (interiors) and environments (exteriors), in other words with the conditions and realities that make people what they are. Moments in the lives of individuals are expanded by the inclusion of all those things which shape and influence them. And it is in Rosswog's photographs of rural interiors – this truly European project – that the fundamental dialectic of human existence is often portrayed in alarming fashion: the pictures show the things people have shaped, and at the same time, the things that have shaped people.

In the early 1980s, Rosswog was a pupil of Professor Bernd Becher at the Düsseldorf Academy of Art. Like most of Becher's pupils, some of whom have meanwhile attained an international reputation, he too has varied the photographic approach of his teacher, and developed it into a creative principle of his own. With all of Becher's pupils, though, a certain formal and thematic relationship can nevertheless still be discerned above and beyond the differences. The large-format landscapes of Thomas Struth, Thomas Ruff's portraits of similarly large dimensions, the townscapes of Boris Becker, the landscapes and interiors of Andreas Gurski and the computer-alienated snapshots of Jörg Sasse all breathe the spirit of realism; their esthetic is determined by a critical dialogue with reality, but at the same time, the beholder is never in danger of confusing the artist with a photo-reporter. Their core content is nothing if not man-made. Martin Rosswog, however, is the only one among the better-known Becher pupils to follow his teacher in his rigorous documentarism. At the same time he is the only one for whom the historical dimension of the works of Bernd Becher and his wife Hilla is a basic function of Rosswog's creative work. Like them, Rosswog works with series, he assembles his pictures into thematic sequences and, like them he is interested in the historical development of a region and of the living conditions of its people. Without the tireless documentary work of the Bechers, the old Ruhr, Germany's former industrial powerhouse, would now be nothing but a part of collective memory; its image would have disappeared. Following the recent decades during which the erstwhile coal-and-steel agglomeration has undergone a decades-long fundamental structural transformation into a decentralized region characterized by service-industries, we would hardly possess any pictorial record of its towns and cities and thus of the living-conditions which four generations of its people experienced.[3] The works of Martin Rosswog are similarly important: his portraits document two decades of western Germany's contemporary history. His rural interiors preserve for all time, in moving and alarming fashion, the travails with which the people of Europe had, and still have, to contend, and how time and again, and evidently everywhere, they reacted with renewed effort to shape and to esthetically furnish their living quarters, to arrange warmth, color and form in a mutual relationship which does justice to the immediate need not only for shelter but also for harmony.

Rural Interiors

Rosswog has been documenting forms of rural living in Europe since 1989. His first journey took him to County Kerry in the south-western corner of Ireland. In the following years he made four more trips there. 1992 saw his first visit to the village of San Martín de la Vega del Alberche in the region of Old Castile in central Spain, to which he has since paid three further visits. In 1995 Rosswog made his first trip to the Häme region of Finland; he has since been to Finland three more times, also visiting the Saimaa region. In fact, he has now visited a total of twelve European countries, recording their rural interiors as documentary works in progress. Alongside the aforementioned regions of Ireland, Spain and Finland, he has visited the Outer Hebrides, off the coast of Scotland, the Memel Delta region of Lithuania, the Karelia region of Russia, the Podhale, Silesia and Podlasie regions of Poland, the Transcarpathia, Kalotaszeg and Ukrainian Carpathia regions of the Ukraine, Transylvania and Maramures in Romania, the Alföd region of Hungary, the Bergisches Land, Oberbergisches Land, Münsterland and Mecklenburg regions of Germany, and Pays de la Loire, Périgord and Creuse regions of France.[4] As a rule, Rosswog selects dwellings occupied by older people, usually the over-sixties. The photographic sessions are largely the result of private contacts, which in turn are arranged through the good offices of local history museums or experts in local customs and history. These contacts facilitate research into subjects for photographs, in addition to helping to create an atmosphere of trust. After all, it should not be forgotten that the inhabitants show this artistic intruder something very intimate: the interior furnishings of a home associated with their innermost emotions.

The Photographer in the Home

Rosswog's procedure can be described using the example of the Spanish village he visited. On a map, San Martín de la Vega del Alberche can be found north of the Sierra de Gredos, 180 kilometers to the west of Madrid. The village lies at 1,500 meters above sea-level; its climate in the summer resembles that of a desert, while its winters are bitterly cold with a lot of snow. On his first visit, Rosswog documented 15 houses, the oldest in the village. Three or four pictures were taken in each house. In addition, he took exterior shots as well as portraits of the inhabitants. Since then, all the older houses in the village have been systematically documented, some two dozen in all. In total, the village has fewer than 100 houses and is home to some 400 people, most of them elderly: "the place is dying", as Rosswog says. The exodus from the countryside, which can be seen throughout Europe, is evident here too: the young people go off to the towns and cities, most of them to Madrid, where they can expect better job opportunities, greater material comforts and the personal freedom that results from urban anonymity. In many cases, city-dwellers are returning to these deserted villages, renovating historic buildings and turning them into weekend or holiday cottages. In San Martín, the two historic mills have been rescued from dereliction in this way, but have become private modern country retreats in the process. This cultural phenomenon can also be observed in County Kerry in Ireland, Creuse in France, the Bergisches Land in Germany and in other rural regions.

A photographic session with Rosswog can last for three hours or longer. During this time the whole dwelling is documented. He takes eight to ten pictures, sometimes more. He has an interpreter to help him communicate with the inhabitants, as well as a folder of his own books and pictures. It is the scientific and documentary aspect of his work which is largely responsible for building trust, creating the opportunity for his artistic activity. Rosswog prefers to take his photographs in the morning, if only because of the natural light essential for his work. The interiors are photographed using a moderately wide-angle lens from the height of a tripod. For his exterior views, he has used a panoramic lens since 1996, producing amazing views of the buildings and their surroundings.

This photographic activity interrupts the daily lives of the inhabitants for several hours. However discreetly the artist behaves, he is the one who dominates the action during this period. The inhabitants withdraw, remain in the background and follow the photographic goings-on either in silence or with a running commentary. For a brief moment, they experience themselves and their world as the objects of someone else's curiosity, which, nevertheless, is focused not on themselves, but on the silent witnesses to their everyday lives: the kitchen sink, the bedsheets, the TV corner, the picture of a saint, the calendar and the dresser. The photographer's activities open up a new aspect in their lives, which they may not previously have recognized. As a result of their house becoming a motif, they step out of their own world for a moment; they find their property taken away from them, yet at the same time reveive a new point of view. The end of the session and the return of the inhabitants to their everyday lives represents a restoration of the situation which all beholders of the pictures in this book must imagine for themselves: the room fills with life once more and the permanent process of creating order and disorder begins afresh.

Pictures between the Pictures

The present book shows Martin Rosswog's documentation "Rural Interiors in Europe" more comprehensively than ever before. The photographer has selected nearly 400 photographs from an archive of several thousand to give a representative impression of the project. The book invites the reader to take a trip through Europe's rural areas, visiting numerous dwellings along the way. The interior photographs are supplemented in many cases by the accompanying exterior views. Initially the latter were seen more as a photographic sketch but since 1994 every house has been photographed from outside as well as inside. Unlike the interiors, which are portrayed in color, the exteriors are always photographed in black and white. This particularly emphasizes the role of the landscape; we learn something of the surroundings, the vicinity of neighboring houses. One by one, the beholder accompanies the photographer through rooms only briefly vacated by their occupants. The captions, which can be found at the beginning of each national section, serve to classify the rooms displayed, and contain information about their function. In addition, the serial arrangement of the pictures provides a further opportunity for orientation. The order often provides a panoramic view, as it were, either within the same room, or progressing from room to room. Often beholders are aided in finding their bearings by the fact that an object appears, seen from different points of view, in several successive pictures – a bed (114, 115, 117), a carpet (238, 241), a wall with a window (344, 345). In this way, every single photograph in this unfolding picture – which is how the photographer describes his ordering principle, as each picture determines the order of the following ones – becomes a kind of seek-and-find game:

little objects on the fringe provide clues to the actual arrangement. This principle is never arbitrary: series of pictures do not result from the chance order in which things are found, but from conscious composition on the part of the artist. In Rosswog's work, each picture points to the next, each view carries another within it, so to speak – and yet each individual picture works quite naturally on its own and develops its own distinct charm. At the same time, when looking at the series, first at the pages lying opposite each other, and then by scanning between them, one continually receives the – intended – impression of a "picture between the pictures". With a little detective instinct, the beholder can succeed in creating a reconstruction which goes beyond the mere depiction. The living spaces, whose real inhabitants are having a siesta out of sight, are populated by the spirit of the searching beholder.

Martin Rosswog's rural interiors make landscape and time visible by inviting comparisons: stoves of similar manufacture (Rayburn, Stanley) can be found for example in Ireland (23) and in Scotland (47); the typical central stove of Finland (88) is also present in the Russian province of Karelia (115). The wooden bars in front of or above the traditional stoves in Finland are used for holding loaves (73), while in Ireland they are used for drying clothes (14), and in Maramureş in Romania they constitute a decorative element for the display of textiles (241).

Art and Science

The scientific ethnological approach behind these pictures is obvious. The photographer's lively curiosity, his eye for details and for atmosphere, makes the total content of the documentation and the project, along with the objects in every single picture, look for all the world like *objets trouvés*, things found by chance. And yet it is precisely this element of chance which ensures the authenticity of the images: the heating and cooking appliances, the dressers, the chairs, the beds. In reality, every one of Martin Rosswog's pictures obeys a severe artistic will, which however is skillfully concealed behind its documentary front. For just as Rosswog has sought and found the dwellings depicted here, he also follows a pre-existent esthetic principle in the selection and arrangement of the pictures. He does not see anything into his scenes which is not there, he does not photograph "beautiful poverty", he does not manipulate anything for the sake of a heightened sense of atmosphere. He always takes his bearings from an existing, discovered esthetic, which he uses as a hook on which to hang his sensitive pictorial compositions. Often the inhabitants tidy up a little before the photographer sets up his tripod. Rosswog has no objection to this because he does not take snapshots but rather seeks to reflect "the esthetic sense of the occupants themselves" as manifested in their feeling for everyday orderliness. Rosswog does not simply portray "old houses" or "old people's houses" but always searches for traces of structured, organized ideas of beauty and order in people's everyday lives. "A striking aspect is an, apparently, archteypal artistic intention on the part of the inhabitants, a desire for creative design in their personal surroundings, using the simplest of means."[5] Rosswog documents a created order, albeit one which never becomes an end in itself, but which, through his photographic "staging" of it, points back to the inhabitants and makes their human dignity visible.

The pleasure felt by the artist is directly conveyed to the beholder through his pictures and in the composition of the series. The artist's highly personal involvement is made visible. For the sensitive and interested beholder, Rosswog's pictures bear a clear signature: the photographer discovers art and conceals it behind a façade of science. This circumstance results naturally enough, in limiting factors where the artist's receptiveness and readiness to work are concerned. In brief, these limiting factors are either an exessive esthetic, or else its total absence. Dereliction and neglect are not documented, for instance. This is not the result of social indifference but because there is no esthetic in dereliction. Rosswog's chief concerns are esthetic and documentary. Yet it goes without saying that a lively social interest speaks from all his pictures. Anyone who observes as closely as Martin Rosswog brings moral categories back into play in his artistic intentions.

The second limiting factor lies at the other end of the scale. The photographic eye capitulates when faced with a surplus of decorative intent, such as Rosswog found in many Hungarian villages. Finally, a third limiting factor points to the historical dimension in the photographer's activity: when the furnishings and fittings of a house become too modern, his interest disappears. The pictures which could then be taken already exist in the catalogues of a major furniture retailers. Many of the interiors that Rosswog has photographed over the years no longer exists in this form (34 – 37, 39, 88, 89). When the inhabitants died, their heirs redecorated and modernized, or else the house is empty and falling into dilapidation. To this extent, Rosswog the photographer is chasing time, albeit not the fleeting present, but the disappearing past. He "rescues" traditional ways of living for posterity; his pictorial archive is the anthropological memory of European rural life.

Romanticism and Realism

This project places Rosswog fairly and squarely in a profoundly romantic tradition, despite the characteristic realism of his work. At the beginning of the 19th century, Achim von Arnim and Clemens Brentano compiled the first-ever collection of German folk-songs, entitled "Des Knaben Wunderhorn" (1805 – 1808), and shortly after (1812 – 1822), the Brothers Grimm published their collection of fairy-tales. Both represented artistic "rescue projects", and both were extraordinarily successful and influential. For many decades to come, they stimulated the literary and ethnologically-interested public in Europe and inspired countless subsequent projects. It is no coincidence that scientific research into "folk culture", and the subsequent rise of the field of study known as "European ethnology" (centering around Wilhelm Heinrich Riehl and others), only established itself in the wake of this intellectual and artistic avant-garde typified by Herder. An artistic eye sharpens the sense of transitoriness. Those who live exclusively in the present lose their memory and eventually themselves.

Hence Rosswog's sources of inspiration are primarily artistic. August Sander's (1870 – 1964) documentation "Menschen des 20. Jahrhunderts" ["Twentieth-century People"][6] influenced his work just as profoundly as the social-documentary photography of Walker Evans (1903 – 1975)[7] or "Die Halligen" – the word denotes the low-lying islands off Germany's north-west coast – by Albert Renger-Patzsch (1897 – 1966)[8], in which the author, unlike in his famous publication "Die Welt ist schön" ["The World is Beautiful"], places his stylistic intention entirely at the service of the documentary cause. Above all, however, Rosswog's inspiration, time and again, comes from the work of the American photographer Paul Strand (1890 – 1976). Strand's documentation "Un paese"[9], in which he portrayed a village in the Po valley in Italy and its inhabitants, or his pictures of the Outer Hebrides[10] off the west coast of Scotland serve as exemplary stimuli for Rosswog's own creativity. In 1954 Strand spent three months on the island of South Uist, which Rosswog also burned to, nearly half a century later. His contact was the son of one of the farmers whom Strand himself had photographed.

Time and again Rosswog has been attracted to cultural "islands": County Kerry in Ireland, where Irish (Gaelic) is still spoken, the houses of German-speaking minorities in Lithuania or Romania, or the relative isolation of the Creuse region, once the poorest *département* in France. The inherent political content which this documentary work inexorably implies can be seen in particular in Rosswog's pictures from Russia and Finland. A comparison of living conditions in the Saimaa region of Finland and in the neighboring Russian republic of Karelia suggests itself both ethnologically and historically, because in Karelia, which was part of Finland until 1940, Rosswog photographed exclusively in formerly Finnish houses. The obligatory large stove, such as can be seen in some of his Finnish pictures (73, 87, 94, 95), had been removed from one of the Russian houses (the base is still visible: 107), and its function is now exercised by an industrially produced replacement. In another house, the traditional Finnish stove has been replaced by central heating and a television made in Russia (108); even so, Finnish stoves can still be found in Karelia (111). On the other hand, old Finnish houses, farmsteads and interiors can still be found today in the formerly Finnish part of Karelia – in contrast to modern Finland where modern affluence has rendered them obsolete. These traces of traditional styles of living are reminiscent, in Rosswog's words, of a double exposure – overlaid by the achievements of socialist production. Using scientific evidence, the artist brings to light the phenomenon of the "concurrence of the non-concurrent", which can be seen as no less than structurally essential for folk culture. Many Finns come face to face with their resettlement trauma by traveling to their former homeland, where they seek out their family farmsteads and make contact with the current inhabitants, most of whom have been resettled there themselves. The traditional division of rooms is still the major common feature: the large combined living, bed and dining room can be found on both sides of the present-day political border (94, 95, 96, 117). Here, everyday things tell the story of human dramas of historic dimensions.

Obstinacy and Self-assertion

The artistic power of Martin Rosswog's pictures is nourished from two sources. One is the "esthetic will", which asserts itself in the face of all resistance. The elaborate arranging of things of everyday use represents, among other things, a struggle against the degradation of poverty. In this sense, Rosswog's pictures are documents of vitality, joy, and self-assertion. Secondly, the pictures are witnesses of an obstinate adherents to old habits and traditions. Even where the available money might run to more efficient stoves, more comfortable beds, more inviting bathrooms, the old furniture and fittings are retained. The rhythm of what one is accustomed to is stronger than the seductive melody of industrial modernity. The photographic and artistic eye for both the backward-looking obstinacy of the people and their forward-looking vitality and self-assertiveness is what gives these pictures by Martin Rosswog their special esthetic quality.

Andreas Graf

1 Rückblende – Befragung einer Generation [Retrospect: Questioning a Generation]. DuMont Buchverlag, Cologne, 1985; Menschenbilder – Porträtfotografien von Martin Rosswog [Pictures of People – Portrait Photographs by Martin Rosswog]. DuMont Buchverlag, Cologne, 1989; Asylbilder [Asylum Pictures]. DuMont Buchverlag, Cologne, 1996

2 Ländliche Innenräume [Rural Interiors]. Schirmer & Mosel, Munich, 1996

3 see e.g. Bernd and Hilla Becher: Hochöfen [Blast Furnaces]. Schirmer & Mosel, Munich, 1990

4 For more details of these regions, see the Plates

5 Brigitte Schlüter: Interieurs – der Blick hinter die Fassaden [Rural Interiors – a Look behind the Façade]. In: Ländliche Innenräume. Schirmer & Mosel, Munich, 1990

6 August Sander: Menschen des 20. Jahrhunderts [20th-century People]. Schirmer & Mosel, Munich, 1980 (reprint)

7 Walker Evans and James Agee: Let us now praise famous men. Houghton Mifflin Company, Boston, 1941

8 Albert Renger-Patzsch: Die Halligen. Introduction by Johann Johannsen. With contributions from Dr Karl Häberlin from Wyk on the island of Föhr. Albertus, Berlin, 1927

9 Paul Strand: Un paese. Text by Cesare Zavattini. Aperture, New York, 1997 (reprint)

10 Paul Strand: Les Hébrides. Text by François Nourissier. Lausanne, 1962. German Edition: Paul Strand, Basil Davidson: Land der Gräser. Die Äußeren Hebriden. VEB Kunst, Dresden, o.J.

Die Kunst erfinden und verbergen

Der Fotograf Martin Rosswog ist ein künstlerischer Dokumentarist. Mit soziologischem Interesse sammelt und bewahrt, archiviert und speichert er, während zugleich sein künstlerischer Blick die Menschen, Gegenstände und Landschaften in ihrer existentiellen Magie aufscheinen lässt. Rosswog zeigt ein Gehöft, eine Schlafstelle, ein Dorf, einen Küchenschrank stets – und das ist im Wortsinn zu verstehen – im eigenen Licht. Seine Kamera spürt die Aura einer Gestalt, eines Gegenstandes auf und bringt ihn von innen heraus zum Leuchten. Niemals verwendet er für seine Aufnahmen künstliche Beleuchtung, dramatische Lichteffekte durch Sonneneinstrahlung werden vermieden. Der Fotograf nimmt keine Zuschreibungen vor, keine Wertungen oder Beurteilungen: Der Künstler mit dem Objektiv ist objektiv. Das bedeutet aber keineswegs, dass er die ästhetische Qualität der abgebildeten Gegenstände nicht offenbart, im Gegenteil: Er holt sie mit Hilfe der Kamera ans Licht. Als Dokumentarist ist Rosswog ein Archivar der verstreichenden Zeit, ein Bibliothekar verloren gehenden Wissens über die Lebensumstände der Menschen, die Verluste der Modernisierung; er ist Beobachter und Aufnehmender, Abwartender. Ein Sammler. Als Künstler dagegen wird er Motor einer Anverwandlung: Die Dinge *sind* nicht, sie *werden* erst durch seinen Blick. Ein Ofen, ein Schrank, eine Vase, ein Telefon: Von Rosswog gesehen, entfalten sie magisches Eigenleben.

Drei große Projekte

Martin Rosswog, 1950 in Bergisch Gladbach bei Köln geboren, arbeitet seit beinahe zwei Jahrzehnten an drei großen fotografischen Projekten, die inhaltlich miteinander verzahnt sind und sich zum Teil bereits in Buchpublikationen niedergeschlagen haben: Porträts von Menschen[1], ländliche Wohnräume[2] und Außenaufnahmen. Diese Reihenfolge gibt auch eine ungefähre zeitliche Abfolge wieder. Das Interesse des Fotografen hat sich allmählich vom einzelnen Menschen zum Menschen als Gruppenwesen verlagert; von der Fixierung des Augenblicks, des Gewordenen (Porträts) ist er schrittweise übergegangen zur Beschäftigung mit den Lebensumständen (Interieurs), der Umgebung (Exterieurs), den Bedingungen und Realitäten, die Menschen zu dem machen, was sie sind. Momente im Leben des Einzelnen wurden erweitert um die Fülle all dessen, was ihn prägt und beeinflusst. Dabei wird gerade bei Rosswogs Fotografien ländlicher Innenräume – diesem wahrhaft europäischen Projekt – die grundlegende Dialektik menschlicher Existenz in oft bestürzender Weise ins Bild gesetzt: Die Bilder zeigen, was der Mensch gemacht, und sie zeigen zugleich, was den Menschen gemacht hat.

Rosswog war Anfang der 1980er Jahre Schüler bei Professor Bernd Becher an der Düsseldorfer Kunstakademie. Wie die meisten Becher-Schüler, von denen einige unterdessen zu internationalem

Ruf gelangt sind, hat auch er die fotografische Vorgehensweise seines Lehrers variiert und zu einem eigenen Gestaltungsprinzip fortentwikkelt. Eine gewisse formale und thematische Verwandtschaft bleibt dennoch über die Verschiedenheiten hinaus bei allen Becher-Schülern erkennbar. Die großformatigen Landschaftsaufnahmen von Thomas Struth und die ebenso groß dimensionierten Porträts eines Thomas Ruff, die Stadtlandschaften von Boris Becker, die Landschaften und Interieurs von Andreas Gursky und auch die PC-verfremdeten Knipsbilder eines Jörg Sasse atmen den Geist des Realismus, ihre Ästhetik wird bestimmt von einer Auseinandersetzung mit der Wirklichkeit, ohne dass der Betrachter je in Verlegenheit käme, die Künstler als Tagesfotografen zu verkennen. Sie alle arbeiten mit höchstem artifiziellen Kerngehalt. Martin Rosswog ist jedoch der einzige unter den bekannten Becher-Schülern, der in ähnlicher Weise wie sein Lehrer konsequent dokumentarisch vorgeht, und er ist zugleich der einzige, für den auch die historische Dimension der Arbeiten Bernd Bechers und seiner Frau Hilla eine grundlegende Funktion des eigenen Schaffens ist. Wie sie arbeitet Rosswog in Serien, er stellt seine Bilder zu thematischen Reihen zusammen, und wie sie ist er interessiert an der geschichtlichen Entwicklung einer Region, der menschlichen Lebensumstände. Ohne die unermüdliche dokumentarische Arbeit der Bechers wäre das alte Ruhrgebiet nur noch Teil des kollektiven Gedächtnisses, sein Bild wäre verschwunden: Nachdem die frühere Kohle- und Stahl-Region einen jahrzehntelangen grundlegenden Strukturwandel zum vielstädtischen Dienstleistungszentrum durchlaufen hat, besäßen wir heute kaum noch ein Bild dieser Städte und damit der Lebensweise der Menschen, die für vier Generationen in dieser Region prägend war.[3] Ähnlich bedeutsam sind die Arbeiten Martin Rosswogs: Seine Porträts dokumentieren zwei Jahrzehnte Zeitgeschichte des westlichen Deutschlands. Und seine ländlichen Innenräume halten für alle Zeiten in bewegender Weise fest, mit welchen Mühsalen die Menschen Europas zu kämpfen hatten und haben, und wie sie darauf, immer wieder und offenbar überall, in stets neuen Anläufen reagieren, ihre Wohnumgebung zu ordnen, ästhetisch einzurichten, Wärme, Farbe und Form in ein Verhältnis zu setzen, das dem unmittelbaren Bedürfnis nach Schutz ebenso gerecht wird wie dem nach Harmonie.

Ländliche Innenräume

Seit 1989 dokumentiert Rosswog ländliche Wohnformen in Europa. Seine erste Reise führte ihn nach Irland, in die im Südwesten der Republik gelegene Region Kerry. In den Jahren danach erfolgten vier weitere Besuche. 1992 war er erstmals Gast in dem spanischen Dorf San Martín de la Vega del Alberche, in der Region Alt-Kastilien im Herzen Spaniens, seitdem hat es drei weitere Besuche gegeben. In die finnische Region Häme reiste Rosswog erstmals 1995, drei weitere Aufenthalte dort bzw. in der Region Saimaa kamen in den Folgejahren hinzu. Mittlerweile hat der Fotograf zwölf europäische Länder besucht und ihre regionale Wohnkultur in ein dokumentarisches „work in progress“ aufgenommen: neben Irland (Region Kerry),

Spanien (Region Alt-Kastilien) und Finnland (Regionen Häme und Saimaa) sind das Schottland (Äußere Hebriden), Litauen (Region Memelland), Russland (Region Karelien), Polen (Regionen Podhale, Schlesien, Podlasie), Ukraine (Regionen Transkarpatien, Kalotaszeg und Ukrainische Karpaten), Rumänien (Regionen Siebenbürgen und Maramures), Ungarn (Region Alföld), Deutschland (Regionen Bergisches Land, Oberbergisches Land, Münsterland und Mecklenburg) und Frankreich (Regionen Pays de la Loire, Périgord und Creuse).[4] In der Regel wählt Rosswog die Wohnungen älterer Menschen aus, die Bewohner haben meist das sechste Lebensjahrzehnt überschritten. Die fotografischen Sitzungen kommen überwiegend durch private Kontakte zustande, die sich ihrerseits über Heimatmuseen vor Ort oder volkskundliche Kenner ergeben. Diese Verbindungen erleichtern die Motivrecherche und dienen einer vorsichtigen Vertrauensbildung. Schließlich offenbaren die Bewohner dem künstlerischen Eindringling im doppelten Wortsinn ihr Innerstes: die Innenausstattung ihrer Wohnung als intimem Ort ihrer Gefühlsbildung.

Der Fotograf im Haus

Rosswogs Vorgehensweise lässt sich am Beispiel des besuchten spanischen Dorfes exemplarisch darstellen. San Martín de la Vega del Alberche findet man auf der Landkarte 180 km westlich von Madrid, nördlich der Sierra de Gredos. Der Ort liegt auf 1500 m Meereshöhe, im Sommer herrscht ein wüstenähnliches Klima, die Winter mit viel Schnee sind bitterkalt. Bei seinem ersten Besuch hat Rosswog 15 Häuser dokumentiert, die ältesten des Ortes. In jedem Haus wurden drei bis vier Aufnahmen gemacht. Dazu kamen Außenaufnahmen sowie Porträts der Bewohner. Seither wurden alle älteren Häuser des Ortes systematisch erfasst, zusammen etwa zwei Dutzend. Der Ort hat insgesamt keine 100 Häuser, dort leben etwa 400 nahezu ausschließlich ältere Einwohner: „ein sterbender Ort“ (Rosswog). Die in ganz Europa zu beobachtende Landflucht ließ auch hier die Jüngeren in die Städte abwandern, meist nach Madrid, wo bessere Arbeitsmöglichkeiten, Wohnkomfort und die Anonymität der Großstadt einen größeren individuellen Freiraum versprechen. Vielfach ziehen nun Städter in die verlassenen Dörfer, renovieren historische Gebäude und nutzen sie als Wochenend- oder Ferienhäuser. In San Martín sind auf diese Weise die zwei historischen Mühlen zwar dem Verfall entgangen, wurden aber in private ländliche Lifestyle-Domizile verwandelt. Auch in Kerry (Irland), der Creuse (Frankreich), dem Bergischen Land (Deutschland) und anderswo ist diese Form des historisierenden Kulturwandels gegenwärtig.

Eine fotografische Sitzung Rosswogs dauert drei Stunden und länger, in ihrem Verlauf wird die Wohnung komplett dokumentiert. Er macht acht bis zehn Aufnahmen, manchmal auch mehr. Bei der Verständigung mit den Bewohnern helfen ihm ein Dolmetscher und eine Mappe mit eigenen Büchern und Bildern. Vor allem der wissenschaftlich-dokumentarische Charakter seiner Arbeiten flößt den Menschen Vertrauen ein und eröffnet den erforderlichen Freiraum für seine künstlerische Tätigkeit. Am liebsten fotografiert Rosswog morgens, schon wegen des natürlichen Lichts, das für seine Bilder unerlässlich ist. Die Innenräume werden mit einem leichten Weitwinkel aus Stativhöhe aufgenommen, für die Außenansichten benutzt er seit 1996 auch eine Panoramakamera, die verblüffende Bildaufschlüsse der Gebäude und Umgebungen liefert.

Für einige Stunden unterbricht die Tätigkeit des Fotografen den Alltag der Hausbewohner. So zurückhaltend der Künstler auch agiert, immer ist doch er es, der für diesen Zeitraum zum Handelnden wird. Die Bewohner ziehen sich zurück, bleiben im Hintergrund, begleiten kommentierend oder stumm die Arbeit des Fotografen. Sie erleben sich und ihre Welt für einen kurzen, irritierenden Moment als Objekte einer Neugier, die sich zwar auf sie bezieht, aber nicht direkt auf ihre Person, sondern auf die stillen Begleiter ihres Alltags, auf Spülbeken und Bettdecke, Fernsehecke, Heiligenbild, Kalender und Geschirrschrank. Die Tätigkeit des Fotografen eröffnet den Bewohnern einen neuen „Wert" ihres Lebens, den sie vorher vielleicht nicht kannten; indem ihre Wohnung zum Objekt wird, treten auch sie für einen Moment aus der eigenen Welt heraus, werden enteignet und zugleich beschenkt. Wenn eine Sitzung beendet ist und die Leute ihren Alltag wieder aufnehmen, beginnt von vorne, was sich der Betrachter zu jedem der Bilder dieses Buches hinzudenken muss: Der Raum füllt sich mit Leben, der fortwährende Prozess des Ordnungschaffens und -zerstörens setzt erneut ein.

Das Bild zwischen den Bildern

Die vorliegende Publikation zeigt Martin Rosswogs Dokumentation „Ländliche Innenräume in Europa" in erstmaliger Ausführlichkeit. Aus einem Archivbestand von mehreren tausend Aufnahmen hat der Fotograf fast 400 Bilder ausgewählt, die einen repräsentativen Eindruck des Projekts vermitteln. Das Buch lädt ein zu einer Rundreise durch Europas ländliche Gegenden, und es erlaubt einen Rundgang durch zahlreiche Wohnungen. Ergänzt werden die Innenansichten häufig durch die zugehörigen Außenaufnahmen. Anfangs eher als fotografische Skizze angelegt, wird seit 1994 jedes Haus außen wie innen aufgenommen. Anders als die farbigen Interieurs sind die Exterieurs jedoch stets in Schwarzweiß gehalten. Vor allem der landschaftliche Aspekt kommt dabei zum Tragen, wir erfahren etwas über die Umgebung, die Nachbarschaft zu anderen Häusern. Raum für Raum geht der Betrachter dann mit dem Fotografen durch die Zimmer, die von ihren Bewohnern nur kurz verlassen wurden. Die Bildlegenden jeweils am Beginn einer Länderstrecke ermöglichen eine klare Zuordnung, sie geben Auskunft über die Funktion der Räume. Darüber hinaus bietet die serielle Anordnung der Bilder eine weitere Orientierungsmöglichkeit: Die Reihenfolge ergibt häufig einen Rundblick, entweder innerhalb des gleichen Raumes oder im Fortschreiten von Zimmer zu Zimmer. Häufig bieten Gegenstände, die auf mehreren hintereinander folgenden Bildern aus unterschiedlichem Blickwinkel zu sehen sind – ein Bett (114, 115, 117), ein Teppich (238, 241), eine gefensterte Wand (344, 345) –, die Möglichkeit, sich zurechtzufinden. Auf diese Weise wird jedes einzelne Bild dieser „Abwicklungen“ – so nennt der Fotograf das Reihungsprinzip, nach dem das vorhergehende Bild die Abfolge des nachfolgenden stiftet – auch zu einem Such-, einem Rätselbild: Kleine Objekte am Rand geben Hinweise auf die reale Anordnung. Das Prinzip der Reihung ist niemals willkürlich: Bildfolgen ergeben sich nicht aus dem Zufall des Vorgefundenen, sondern zwingend aus der Komposition durch den Fotografen. Bei Rosswog weist jedes Bild immer schon auf das nächste hin, jede Ansicht trägt gleichsam eine weitere in sich – und dennoch funktioniert jedes Einzelbild wie selbstverständlich auch für sich selbst und entwickelt seinen ganz eigenen Reiz. Zugleich entsteht beim Betrachten der Serien – zunächst der jeweils gegenüberliegenden Seiten, dann aber auch beim Blättern zwischen diesen – immer wieder der beabsichtigte Eindruck eines „Bildes zwischen den Bildern“. Mit ein wenig detektivischem Spürsinn gelingt dem Betrachter eine Rekonstruktion über die reine Abbildung hinaus. Die Wohnräume, deren wirkliche Bewohner unsichtbar Siesta halten, bevölkern sich mit dem Geist des forschenden Beobachters.

Martin Rosswogs ländliche Innenräume machen Landschaft und Zeit sichtbar, indem sie zum Vergleich einladen: Öfen ähnlicher Bauart (Rayburn, Stanley) finden sich beispielsweise in Irland (23) wie in Schottland (47), der typische zentral gelegene Ofen Finnlands (88) ist auch im russischen Karelien noch präsent (115), die hölzernen Stangen vor oder über den traditionellen Öfen dienen in Finnland zur Aufbewahrung von Broten (73), in Irland trocknet man daran Kleidungsstücke (14), und im rumänischen Maramures werden sie zu einem dekorativen Element, das Textilien zur Schau stellt (241).

Kunst und Wissenschaft

Der volkskundliche, wissenschaftliche Ansatz dieser Bilder liegt auf der Hand. Die wache Neugier des Fotografen, sein Blick für Details, für Atmosphärisches lässt mit selbstverständlicher Leichtigkeit den gesamten Inhalt der Dokumentation, des Projektes und die Gegenstände jedes einzelnen Bildes als Fundstücke, als zufällig und schon deshalb „wahr“ erscheinen: die Öfen und Kochgelegenheiten, die Geschirrschränke, Sitzecken und Betten. In Wirklichkeit gehorcht jedes einzelne Bild von Martin Rosswog einem strengen künstlerischen Willen, der sich jedoch im Dokumentarischen geschickt zu verbergen weiß. Denn wie Rosswog die abgebildeten Wohnungen gesucht und gefunden hat, so folgt er auch in Bildauswahl und Bildaufbau einem vorhandenen, einem vorgefundenen ästhetischen Prinzip. Er sieht nichts in die Wohnungen „hinein“, er fotografiert kein „schönes Elend“, er manipuliert nichts, um eine höhere Stimmigkeit zu erzeugen. Häufig räumen die Bewohner ein wenig auf, bevor der Fotograf sein Stativ aufbaut. Das ist durchaus im Sinn Rosswogs, der keine Momentaufnahmen produziert, sondern „das ästhetische Empfinden der Bewohner“ abbildet, wie es sich in der alltäglichen Ordnung manifestiert. Rosswog lichtet nicht einfach „alte Wohnungen“ oder „Wohnungen alter Leute“ ab, sondern er ist immer auch auf der Suche nach Spuren von Ordnungs- und Schönheitsvorstellungen im

Alltag der Menschen. „Auffallend ist ein anscheinend archetypisches Kunstwollen der Bewohner, der Wille zur kreativen Ausgestaltung des persönlichen Wohnumfeldes mit einfachsten Mitteln".[5] Rosswog dokumentiert eine hergestellte Ordnung, die allerdings niemals einen Selbstzweck erfüllt, sondern die, indem er sie fotografisch „inszeniert", immer auf die Bewohner zurückverweist und deren menschliche Würde sichtbar macht.

Die Lust des Künstlers teilt sich dem Betrachter in seinen Bildern und den zusammengestellten Reihen unmittelbar mit. Die ganz persönliche Beteiligung des Künstlers, seine Handschrift, wird sichtbar. Rosswogs Bilder tragen für den einfühlsamen und interessierten Beobachter eine deutliche Signatur: Der Fotograf findet die Kunst und verbirgt sie hinter der Wissenschaft. Aus diesem Umstand ergeben sich naturgemäß limitierende Faktoren für Aufnahmebereitschaft und Einsatzwillen des Künstlers. Dies sind, kurz gesagt, entweder eine gegen Null strebende Ästhetik oder deren Übermaß. Verwahrlosung etwa wird nicht dokumentiert, und zwar nicht aus sozialem Desinteresse. Aber vor der Verwahrlosung flüchtet die Ästhetik. Rosswogs Hauptanliegen ist ein ästhetisch-archivarisches. Dennoch spricht aus seinen Bildern selbstverständlich ein waches soziales Interesse. Wer so genau zu beobachten weiß wie Martin Rosswog, der bringt moralische Kategorien in seinem künstlerischen Wollen zurück ins Spiel.

Die zweite Grenze liegt am anderen Ende der Skala. Auch vor einem überbordenden Ausschmückungswillen, wie er dem Künstler etwa in manchen ungarischen Örtlichkeiten begegnete, kapituliert das fotografische Auge. Ein dritte Grenze schließlich verweist auf die historische Dimension in der Tätigkeit des Fotografen: Wenn die Ausstattung der Wohnungen zu modern wird, verliert sich sein Interesse. Die Bilder, die dann entstehen könnten, existieren bereits in den Katalogen der großen Möbelhäuser.

Manche Wohnungen, die Rosswog im Lauf der Jahre dokumentiert hat, existieren heute bereits nicht mehr in dieser Weise (34-37, 39, 88, 89). Ihre Bewohner sind verstorben, die Erben haben renoviert, erneuert, modernisiert, oder das Haus steht leer und verfällt. Insofern läuft Rosswog als Fotograf der Zeit hinterher, jedoch nicht der flüchtigen Gegenwart, sondern der verschwindenden Vergangenheit. Er „rettet" die traditionellen Wohnformen für die Nachwelt, sein Bildarchiv ist das anthropologische Gedächtnis der europäischen Ländlichkeit.

Romantik und Realismus

Mit diesem Projekt befindet sich der realistische Künstler Rosswog in einer zutiefst romantischen Tradition. Arnim und Brentano veröffentlichten am Beginn des 19. Jahrhunderts mit „Des Knaben Wunderhorn" (1805 – 1808) erstmals eine Sammlung deutscher Volkslieder, und die Brüder Grimm gaben kurz darauf ihre Sammlung der „Kinder- und Hausmärchen" (1812 – 1822) heraus, beide künstlerische „Rettungsprojekte", und beide äußerst erfolg- und einflussreich: Sie befruchteten für viele Jahrzehnte die philologische und ethnologische Öffentlichkeit in ganz Europa und regten unzählige

Nachfolgeprojekte an. Es ist kein Zufall, dass sich die wissenschaftliche Erforschung des Gegenstandes „Volkskultur" – mit der Entstehung des heute als „europäische Ethnologie" bezeichneten Faches (um Wilhelm Heinrich Riehl und andere) – erst in der Nachfolge dieser künstlerischen und intellektuellen Avantgarde (Herder) etablierte. Der künstlerische Blick schärft das Gespür für die Zeitlichkeit und ihre Verluste. Wer ausschließlich in der Gegenwart lebt, verliert sein Gedächtnis und am Ende sich selbst.

So sind denn auch die Inspirationsquellen des Künstlers Rosswog zunächst künstlerische. August Sanders (1870–1964) Dokumentation „Menschen des 20. Jahrhunderts"[6] hat bei seinen Arbeiten ebenso Pate gestanden wie die sozialdokumentarische Fotografie eines Walker Evans (1903–1975)[7] oder das Werk „Die Halligen" von Albert Renger-Patzsch (1897–1966)[8], für das dieser seinen Stilwillen, anders als in der berühmten Publikation „Die Welt ist schön", vollständig in den Dienst an der dokumentarischen Sache stellte. Vor allem aber sind es immer wieder Arbeiten des amerikanischen Fotografen Paul Strand (1890–1976), an die Rosswog anknüpft. Strands Dokumentation „Un paese"[9], in der er ein Dorf in der italienischen Po-Ebene und seine Bewohner vorstellte, oder seine Bilder von den Äußeren Hebriden (Schottland)[10] sind Rosswog Vorbild und Anreiz für die eigene Kreativität. Strand hatte 1954 drei Monate auf South Uist gelebt, wohin sich nahezu ein halbes Jahrhundert später auch Martin Rosswog wendete. Seine Kontaktperson dort war der Sohn eines Bauern, den Strand seinerzeit fotografiert hatte.

Immer wieder sind es kulturelle „Inseln", die das Interesse Rosswogs auf sich ziehen: das irische Kerry, wo noch Gälisch gesprochen wird, die Wohnungen deutschsprachiger Minderheiten in Litauen oder Rumänien oder die relative Abgeschiedenheit der Creuse als einstmals ärmstem Departement Frankreichs. Der immanente politische Gehalt, der mit solcher Dokumentationsarbeit unweigerlich einhergeht, zeigt sich besonders deutlich in Rosswogs Bildern aus Russland und Finnland. Ein Vergleich der Wohnverhältnisse in der finnischen Region Saimaa und der russischen Region Karelien liegt ethnologisch wie historisch nahe, da Rosswog in Karelien, das bis 1940 zu Finnland gehörte, ausschließlich in ehemals finnischen Wohnungen fotografiert hat. Der obligatorische große Ofen, wie er auf einigen finnischen Bildern zu sehen ist (73, 87, 94, 95), wurde in einer Wohnung in Russland entfernt (das Fundament ist noch sichtbar: 107) und ein Industrieofen übernimmt seine Funktion. In einer anderen Wohnung ersetzen eine Zentralheizung und ein Fernseher sowjetischer Bauart (108) den Ofen finnischer Tradition, der aber auch in Karelien noch zu finden ist (111). Im ehemals finnischen Teil Kareliens finden sich heute gleichwohl altfinnische Häuser, Anwesen und Interieurs, wie es sie in Finnland selbst aufgrund der Wohlstandsentwicklung nicht mehr gibt. Diese Spuren traditionellen Wohnens sind gleichsam „wie bei einer Doppelbelichtung" (Rosswog) überlagert von den Errungenschaften der sozialistischen Warenwelt. Das Phänomen von der „Gleichzeitigkeit des Ungleichzeitigen", das für die Volkskultur als geradezu strukturbildend anzusehen ist, wird vom Künstler mit wissenschaftlicher Evidenz ins Bild gesetzt. Ihrem Umsiedlungstrauma begegnen viele Finnen mit Reisen in ihre ehemalige Heimat, wo sie die Familiengehöfte aufsuchen und Kontakt pflegen zu den jetzigen Bewohnern, meist selbst Umgesiedelten. Am ehesten zeigt noch die traditionelle Raumaufteilung Gemeinsamkeiten: Der große Wohn-, Schlaf- und Essraum findet sich diesseits wie jenseits der heutigen politischen Grenze (94, 95, 96, 117). Hier erzählen die Dinge des Alltags von menschlichen Dramen historischer Dimension.

Beharrungs- und Behauptungswille

Die künstlerische Kraft der Bilder von Martin Rosswog speist sich vor allem aus zwei Quellen. Zum einen aus dem „Willen zur Ästhetik", der sich allen Widerständen zum Trotz behauptet. Das kunstvolle Ordnen der Dinge des täglichen Bedarfs stellt einen Kampf dar gegen die Entwürdigungen der Armut. Insofern sind Rosswogs Bilder Dokumente von Lebenskraft, Freude und Behauptungswillen. Zum anderen sind die Bilder Zeugnisse einer Verbundenheit mit überlieferten Traditionen. Selbst dort, wo vielleicht das Geld für leistungskräftigere Öfen, bequemere Betten, behaglichere Bäder vorhanden wäre, bleibt'es beim Althergebrachten. Der Rhythmus des Gewohnten ist stärker als die verführerische Melodie der industrialisierten Moderne. Der fotografisch-künstlerische Blick für beides, das eher rückwärts gewandte Beharrungsvermögen der Menschen und den vorwärts blickenden Lebens- und Behauptungswillen, verleiht den Bildern von Martin Rosswog ihre eigene bedeutungsvolle Ästhetik.

Andreas Graf

1 Rückblende – Befragung einer Generation. DuMont Buchverlag, Köln, 1985; Menschenbilder – Porträtfotografien von Martin Rosswog. DuMont Buchverlag, Köln, 1989; Asylbilder. DuMont Buchverlag, Köln, 1996

2 Ländliche Innenräume. Schirmer & Mosel, München, 1996

3 Vgl. z.B. Bernd und Hilla Becher: Hochöfen. Schirmer & Mosel, München, 1990

4 Genauere Angaben zu den Regionen finden sich in den Tafeln

5 Brigitte Schlüter: Interieurs – der Blick hinter die Fassaden. In: Ländliche Innenräume. Schirmer & Mosel, München, 1990

6 August Sander: Menschen des 20. Jahrhunderts. Schirmer & Mosel, München, 1980 (Nachdruck)

7 Walker Evans / James Agee: Let us now praise famous men. Houghton Mifflin Company, Boston, 1941

8 Albert Renger-Patzsch: Die Halligen. Geleitwort von Johann Johannsen. Unter Mitwirkung von Dr. Karl Häberlin in Wyk auf Föhr. Albertus, Berlin, 1927

9 Paul Strand: Un paese. Text von Cesare Zavattini. Aperture, New York, 1997 (Nachdruck)

10 Paul Strand: Les Hébrides. Text von Francois Nourissier. Lausanne, 1962. Dt. Ausgabe: Paul Strand, Basil Davidson: Land der Gräser. Die Äußeren Hebriden. VEB Kunst, Dresden, o.J.

Inventer et dissimuler l'art

Le photographe Martin Rosswog est un artiste documentariste. Tandis qu'il rassemble, collectionne, archive et mémorise à la manière d'un sociologue, simultanément son regard d'artiste fait apparaître êtres humains, objets et paysages dans leur magie existentielle. Qu'il s'agisse d'une ferme, d'un gîte, d'un village ou d'un buffet de cuisine, Rosswog les présente toujours – au sens propre du terme – baignés de leur propre lumière. Sa caméra perçoit l'aura d'une silhouette ou d'un objet et les fait briller de l'intérieur. Pour ses prises de vue, jamais il n'utilise d'éclairage artificiel et il évite les effets de lumière dramatiques provenant du rayonnement solaire. Le photographe ne fait aucun supputation, aucune appréciation, ne porte aucune jugement: l'artiste muni d'un objectif est objectif. Mais cela ne signifie aucunement qu'il ne révèle pas la qualité esthétique des objets représentés, au contraire: à l'aide de son appareil photo, il la dévoile. En tant que documentariste, Rosswog est un archiviste du temps qui passe, un bibliothécaire de connaissances, en train de sombrer dans l'oubli, sur des modes de vie des hommes ou des passifs de la modernisation; il observe, recueille et patiente. Un collectionneur. En tant qu'artiste, Rosswog devient en revanche le moteur d'une métamorphose: les choses ne sont pas, c'est uniquement à partir de son regard qu'elles deviennent. Un poêle, une armoire, un vase, un téléphone: vus par Rosswog ils s'animent avec magie.

Trois grands projets

Né en 1950 à Bergisch Gladbach, près de Cologne, Martin Rosswog travaille depuis presque vingt ans sur trois grands projets photographiques liés par leur contenu et qui figurent déjà en partie dans trois publications: des portraits de personnes[1], des photographies d'intérieurs ruraux[2] et des extérieurs. Cet ordre correspond aussi à une chronologie approximative. L'intérêt du photographe s'est éloigné peu à peu de l'individu pour se reporter sur l'être social; de la fixation de l'instantané, de ce qui est devenu (portraits), il s'est tourné progressivement vers l'étude des conditions de vie (intérieurs), de l'environnement proche (extérieurs), des conditions et réalités qui font de l'homme ce qu'il est. Des moments de la vie de personnes individuelles ont été enrichis par la profusion de tout ce qui les marque et les influence. C'est en cela que précisément les photographies d'intérieurs ruraux de Rosswog – un projet d'une réelle dimension européenne – révèlent de manière souvent bouleversante la dialectique fondamentale de l'existence humaine: les photos montrent ce que l'homme a fait en même temps que ce qui a fait l'homme.

Rosswog suivi les cours du professeur Bernd Becher à l'École des Beaux-Arts de Düsseldorf au début des années 1980. À l'instar de la plupart des disciples de Becher – dont certains jouissent à présent d'une renommée internationale –, il a varié le procédé photographique de son maître et l'a perfectionné pour accéder à son propre principe de création. On reconnaît cependant une certaine parenté formelle et thématique par-delà les différences chez tous les élèves de Becher. Les paysages grand format de Thomas Struth et les portraits géants d'un Thomas Ruff, les sites urbains de Boris Becker, les paysages et intérieurs d'Andreas Gursky ou encore les instantanés traités par ordinateur de Jörg Sasse sont tous dans l'esprit du Réalisme, leur esthétique est déterminée par la confrontation à la réalité, sans pour autant que l'observateur ne soit tenté de voir dans l'artiste un simple photographe. Tous travaillent à partir d'une substance extrêmement artificielle. Martin Rosswog est toutefois le seul, parmi les disciples connus de Becher, à travailler – comme son maître – rigoureusement suivant le principe du documentaire. Il est également le seul artiste pour qui la dimension historique des travaux de Bernd Becher et de son épouse Hilla joue un rôle fondamental dans sa propre création. Comme eux, Rosswog travaille par séries, assemble ses photos en suites thématiques, et comme eux encore, il s'intéresse au développement historique d'une région, au cadre de vie humain. Sans l'infatigable travail documentaire des époux Becher, le vieux bassin de la Ruhr ne serait plus qu'une partie de la mémoire collective, son image aurait disparu. Après des décennies de restructuration radicale qui ont transformé l'ancienne région du charbon et de l'acier en un centre polyurbain du secteur tertiaire, nous aurions à peine idée de ce qu'étaient jadis ces villes et du mode de vie caractéristique sur quatre générations dans cette région.[3] Les travaux de Martin Rosswog ont une importance comparable: ses portraits racontent vingt ans de l'histoire contemporaine de l'Allemagne de l'Ouest. Ses intérieurs ruraux retiennent à jamais, de manière émouvante, combien les hommes en Europe ont eu à se battre douloureusement et se battent encore, et comment ils se remettent, sans cesse et manifestement partout, à ordonner de neuf leur habitat, à l'aménager esthétiquement et à trouver un équilibre entre chaleur, couleur et forme de manière à satisfaire un besoin immédiat de protection autant que par souri d'harmonie.

Intérieurs ruraux

Rosswog s'attache depuis 1989 à documenter des formes d'habitat rural en Europe. Son premier voyage le conduit en Irland, dans le Kerry situé dans le sud-oest de la République. Il s'y rendra encore quatre fois par la sinte. En 1992, il séjourne pour la première fois dans le village espagnol de San Martín de la Vega del Alberche, en Vielle-Castille, au cœur de l'Espagne, où il retournera trois fois. Il parcourt la région finlandaise de Häme pour la première fois en 1995, il y fera trois autres séjours les années suivantes et ira également dans la région de Saimaa. Entre-temps, le photographe a visité douze pays européens et constitué une documentation sous forme de «work in progress» de leur habitat régional: Irlande (Kerry), Espagne (Vielle-Castille), Finlande (régions de Häme et Saimaa), puis Écosse (Hébrides extérieures), Lituanie (région de Klaipëda), Russie (Carélie), Pologne (régions de Podhale, de Silésie et de Podlasie), Ukraine

(Transcarpatie, Kalotaszeg et Carpates ukrainiennes), Roumanie (Transylvanie et Maramures), Hongrie (région de l'Alföld), Allemagne (pays de Berg, d'Oberberg, du bassin de Münster et du Mecklembourg) et, enfin, France (Pays de la Loire, Périgord et Creuse).[4] Rosswog photographie généralement les habitations de personnes âgées, c'est-à-dire ayant pour la plupart dépassé la soixantaine. Les séances photographiques ont lieu essentiellement grâce à des contacts privés, établis par l'intermédiaire de musées régionaux ou de gens connaissant bien la culture régionale. Ces relations facilitent la recherche de motifs et permettent de gagner prudemment la confiance des habitants. Finalement, ces derniers révèlent à l'artiste intrus ce qu'ils ont de plus intime – au sens double des terme –: l'aménagement de leur intérieur, en tant que sanctuaire de leur vie affective.

Un photographe dans la maison

La visite du village espagnol illustre de manière exemplaire la méthode de Rosswog. Sur la carte, San Martín de la Vega del Alberche se trouve à 180 km à l'ouest de Madrid, au nord de la Sierra de Gredos, perché à 1500 m d'altitude; l'été, il y règne un climat quasi désertique alors que les hivers sont très enneigés et extrêmement froids. Lors de son premier séjour, Rosswog a documenté 15 maisons, les plus anciennes de la localité. Dans chacune, il a réalisé trois ou quatre clichés, auxquels sont venus s'ajouter des photos d'extérieur ainsi que des portraits des habitants. Ensuite, toutes les maisons plus anciennes de la localité ont été saisies systématiquement, soit environ 24 au total. Le village compte à peine 100 maisons en tout, habitées par quelque 400 personnes, presque uniquement des gens âgés: «un village à l'agonie», dit Rosswog. L'exode rural, un phénomène observable un peu partout en Europe, a engendré l'emigration des plus jeunes vers les villes, le plus souvent vers Madrid, où de meilleures perspectives de travail, un habitat plus confortable et l'anonymat de la grande ville promettent une plus grande liberté individuelle. Aujourd'hui, de nombreux citadins emménagent dans les villages abandonnés et rénovent les bâtiments anciens en résidences secondaires. À San Martín, les deux moulins historiques ont pu être ainsi sauvés de la ruine au prix d'une transformation en maison de campagne moderne. Cette évolution culturelle historisante s'opère également dans le Kerry (Irlande), en Creuse (France), dans le Berg (Allemagne) et ailleurs.

Au cours d'une séance photographique qui dure souvent trois heures et plus, Rosswog réalise une documentation complète de l'habitation. Il prend huit à dix photos, parfois plus. Pour communiquer avec les habitants, il recourt aux services d'un interprète ainsi qu'à des livres et des photographies personnels. Notamment le caractère scientifique-documentaire de ses travaux inspire confiance aux gens et laisse à son activité artistique la marge de liberté dont elle a besoin. Rosswog préfère photographier le matin, ne serait-ce que pour bénéficier de la lumière naturelle indispensable à ses travaux. Il photographie les intérieurs avec un appareil à objectif légèrement grand angulaire posé sur un trépied; pour les extérieurs il utilise depuis 1996 un objectif panoramique qui permet de réaliser des photos stupéfiantes des bâtiments et de leur environnement.

L'activité du photographe interrompt pendant quelques heures le quotidien des habitants. En dépit de toute sa discrétion, c'est lui l'acteur durant ce laps de temps. Les occupants de la maison se retirent, restent à l'arrière-plan, commentent ou suivent en silence le travail du photographe. Pour un court et irritant instant, ils se sentent – avec leur environnement – l'objet d'une curiosité qui, bien que dirigée sur eux, se focalise non pas directement sur leur personne mais plutôt sur les compagnons muets de leur quotidien – lavabo et dessus de lit, coin télévision, image sainte, calendrier ou buffet. L'activité du photographe révèle, aux habitants une nouvelle «valeur» de leur vie, qu'ils ignoraient peut-être auparavant; tandis que leur logement devient un objet d'étude, ils sortent un instant de leur propre monde, sont dépossédés et comblés à la fois. Lorsque la séance se termine et que le quotidien reprend ses droits, recommence de zéro ce que l'observateur doit imaginer devant chaque photographie de ce livre: la pièce se remplit de vie et le processus continuel de mise en ordre et en désordre se ré-enclenche.

L'image entre les images

Cet ouvrage présente, de manière inédite et détaillée, la documentation de Martin Rosswog «Intéreiurs ruraux en Europe». Le photographe a sélectionné presque 400 photos – parmi les plusieurs milliers d'images que contiennent ses archives – représentatives de l'ensemble de son projet. Ce livre invite à parcourir des régions rurales d'Europe et à visiter de nombreuses habitations. Les vues d'intérieurs sont souvent complétées par celles des extérieurs qui leur correspondent. Plutôt conçue comme une esquisse photographique au début, à partir de 1994 chaque maison est photographiée de l'intérieur comme de l'extérieur. Contrairement aux intérieurs, en couleur, les extérieurs sont toujours en noir et blanc. Cela met en valeur l'aspect rural et informe sur le voisinage immédiat des maisons. L'observateur accompagne le photographe d'une pièce à l'autre, dont les habitants ne sont sortés que pour un court instant. Les légendes au début d'une série sur un pays permettent un agencement clair, renseignent sur la fonction des pièces. Par ailleurs, la classification sérielle des photographies constitue un moyen d'orientation supplémentaire: la suite de photos offre souvent une vue panoramique soit à l'intérieur d'une même pièce soit en travelling de l'une à l'autre. Souvent, des objets photographiés successivement sous des angles différents – un lit (114, 115, 117), un tapis (238, 241), un mur percé d'une fenêtre (344, 345). Ainsi, chaque élément de ces «déroulages» – terme adopté par le photographe pour qualifier le principe de sérialisation où l'image suivante est la suite logique de la précédente – devient également un rébus: de petits objets en marge fournissent des indications sur l'ordonnancement réel. Ce principe de sérialisation n'est jamais arbitraire: le succession des photos ne résulte pas incidemment de ce que l'on découvre, mais impérativement de la composition voulue par le photographe. Chez Rosswog, chaque photographie annonce déjà la prochaine – chaque vue en recèle une autre en même temps – et malgré tout, chacune a individuellement, et comme logiquement, sa propre fonction et son propre charme. Lorsque l'on regarde une belle série – en commençant par les pages doubles, puis en feuillant page par page – on a sans cesse – et c'est d'ailleurs l'intention de Rosswog – l'impression de voir une «photo entre les photos». Avec un peu de perspicacité, l'observateur parvient à faire une reconstitution allant au – delà de l'illustration. L'esprit de l'observateur curieux investit les pièces dont les véritables occupants se sont retirés pour faire le sieste.

En incitant à comparer, les intérieurs ruraux de Martin Rosswog visualisent le paysage et le temps: par exemple, on retrouve des poêles de style pareil (Rayburn, Stanley) en Irlande (23) et en Écosse (47); le poêle placé au milieu d'une pièce comme c'est l'usage en Finlande (88) est également présent de nos jours en Carélie russe (115); tandis que les barres en bois placées devant ou sur les poêles traditionnels en Finlande servent à la conservation du pain (73), en Irlande on fait sécher les vêtements dessus (14) et dans la région de Maramures en Roumanie (241) elles sont un élément décoratif sur lequel on expose les textiles.

L'art et la science

L'approche ethnologique scientifique de ces photographies est évidente. La curiosité aiguë du photographe, sa capacité de saisir le détail et l'atmosphère transforment avec une légèreté évidente le contenu entier de cette documentation, du projet et les objets de chaque photo en objets trouvés, fortuits, qui par là même en deviennent «authentiques»: fourneaux et poêles, buffets, coins salon et lits. En vérité, chaque photographie de Martin Rosswog obéit à une sévère volonté artistique qui réussit cependant à disparaître habilement derrière le documentaire. De la même manière qu'il a cherché et trouvé les habitations photographiées, Rosswog suit également un principe esthétique donné pour sélectionner et ordonner ses photos. Son regard n'ajoute rien aux habitations, il ne photographie pas de «belle détresse» ne manipule rien pour créer plus d'harmonie. Souvent, les habitants font un peu de rangement avant que le photographe n'installe son trépied. Cela convient parfaitement à Rosswog qui ne cherche pas à produire des instantanés mais à photographier «le sens de l'esthétique des habitants» tel qu'il se manifeste dans leur quotidien. Rosswog ne photographie pas simplement de «vielles habitations» ou des «habitations de personnes âgées»: il est toujours à la recherche d'indices qui renseignent sur la conception de l'ordre et de l'esthétique de la vie quotidienne des gens. «Ce qui frappe, c'est le souci artistique apparemment archétypique des habitants, leur volonté de décorer leur environnement proche avec les moyens les plus simples».[5] Rosswog documente un ordre déjà en place qu'il n'utilise jamais à ses propres fins mais qui, «mis en scène» avec l'appareil photo, renvoie toujours aux habitants et rend visible leur dignité.

Le plaisir de l'artiste se transmet à l'observateur directement à partir des photos et des séries réalisées. L'implication toute personnelle de l'artiste, sa griffe, devient visible. Pour l'observateur sensible et intéressé les photographies de Rosswog portent une signature nette: le photographe découvre l'art et le dissimule derrière la science. D'où des facteurs qui limitent naturellement la réceptivité de l'artiste et sa volonté de s'engager. Il s'agit, en somme, soit d'une esthétique proche de zéro soit d'un excès d'esthétique. Le laisser-aller n'est jamais documenté, non par désintérêt social mais parce qu'il fait fuir l'esthétique. L'intérêt principal de Rosswog c'est de documenter l'esthétique. Néanmoins, des photos de Rosswog émane avec évidence un vif intérêt social. Un maître de l'observation tel que Rosswog réintroduit toujours des valeurs morales dans sa volonté artistique.

La deuxième limite se situe exactement à l'opposé. Face également à un effort de décoration excessif, comme celui que l'artiste a vu dans de nombreuses localités hongroises, l'œil du photographe capitule. Une troisième limite enfin renvoie à la dimension historique de l'activité du photographe: lorsque son ameublement est trop moderne, une habitation perd de son intérêt. Les images qui pourraient en résulter existent déjà dans les catalogues des grandes maisons d'ameublement. Maints logements documentés au fil des années par si n'existent déjà plus tels quels (34-37, 39, 88, 89). Leurs occupants sont décédés et leurs héritiers ont rénové, remplacé, modernisé, ou bien la maison a été abandonnée et tombe en ruines. C'est en cela que Rosswog court après le temps, non pas à la poursuite du présent éphémère mais plutôt du passé en train de disparaître. Il «sauvegarde» les formes traditionnelles d'habitat pour les générations futures, ses images d'archive sont la mémoire anthropologique du monde rural européen.

Romantisme et réalisme

Avec ce projet, Rosswog – artiste réaliste – se meut dans une tradition hautement romantique. Avec «Le Cor enchanté de l'enfant» (1805–1808), publié au début du XIXe siècle, Achim von Arnim et Clemens Brentano sont les premiers à présenter un recueil de chansons populaires allemandes, bientôt suivis par les frères Grimm et leur recueil «contes d'enfants et du foyer» (1812–1822), deux «projets de sauvetage» par l'art extrêmement connus et influents: ils ont enrichi pendant plusieurs siècles la publication philologique et ethnologique de toute l'Europe et inspiré d'innombrables projets ultérieurs. Ce n'est pas un hasard si l'étude scientifique de l'objet «culture populaire» – avec l'émergence de ce qu'on appelle aujourd'hui «l'ethnologie européenne» (autour de Wilhelm Heinrich Riehl et d'autres) – s'est établie seulement à la suite de ce mouvement de l'avant-garde artistique et intellectuelle (Herder). La vision artistique acère l'intuition de la temporalité et de ses passifs. Celui qui vit uniquement dans le temps présent perd la mémoire et finit par se perdre lui-même. Les sources d'inspiration de Rosswog l'artiste sont d'abord de nature artistique. «Visage de ce temps»[6], d'August Sander (1870–1964) aura autant influencé son travail que la photographie socio-documentaire d'un Walker Evans (1903–1975)[7] ou l'ouvrage

«Die Halligen» d'Albert Renger-Patzsch (1897–1966)[8], dans lequel celui-ci mettait toute sa volonté stylistique, autrement que dans sa célèbre publication «Le monde est beau», au service de la cause documentariste. Mais c'est toujours le travail du photographe américain Paul Strand (1890–1976) que Rosswog prend comme point de départ. La documentation de Strand, «Un paese»[9], dans laquelle il présentait un village de la plaine du Pô, en Italie, et ses habitants, ou alors ses photographies des Hébrides extérieures (Écosse)[10] servent à Rosswog de modèle et de moteur pour sa propre créativité. Martin Rosswog se rend, presque cinquante ans plus tard, sur l'île de Sud Uist où Brand a vécu trois mois en 1954. Il a pour contact le fils d'un des paysans photographiés à l'époque par Strand.

Ce sont toujours des «îles» culturelles qui attirent l'attention de Rosswog: le comté irlandais du Kerry où l'on parle encore le gaélique, les habitations des minorités germanophones en Lituanie et en Roumanie, ou bien la Creuse, département relativement isolé qui fut l'un des plus pauvres de France. Le contenu politique immanent, qui se couple inéluctablement à ce genre de travail documentaire, est particulièrement net dans les photographies de Rosswog en Russie et en Finlande. Une comparaison tant ethnologique qu'historique s'etablit logiquement puisqu'en Carélie, rattachée à la Finlande jusqu'en 1940, Rosswog n'a photographié que d'anciennes habitations finlandaises. Le grand poêle de rigueur que l'on voit sur quelques photographies de Finlande (73, 87, 94, 95) a disparu d'une habitation russe (le socle est encore apparent, 107): remplacé par un poêle industriel. Dans une autre demeure, le chauffage central et un téléviseur de fabrication soviétique (108) se subsistuent au poêle finlandais traditionnel, encore présent ailleurs en Carélie (111). Dans la partie de Carélie autrefois finlandaise, on trouve de vieux domaines, maisons et intérieurs finlandais qui n'existent plus en Finlande en raison de la prospérité croissante. Sur ces vestiges d'habitat traditionnel viennent se coller «à l'instar d'une surimpression» (Rosswog) les acquis du monde de la consommation socialiste. Le phénomène de la «simultanéité du non-simultané», perçu précisément comme structurant pour la culture populaire, est mis en un avant par l'artiste avec une évidence scientifique. Nombre de Finlandais combattent le traumatisme de leur «décolonisation» en retournant dans leur ancienne patrie pour revoir leurs anciennes propriétés de famille, en entretenant le contact avec les occupants actuels, eux-mêmes pour la plupart une population déplacée. C'est dans la répartition traditionnelle des pièces qu'on trouve le plus de points communs: la grande pièce servant à la fois de salle de séjour, de salle à manger et de chambre à coucher – transcende ici comme là-bas le frontière politique actuelle (94, 95, 96, 117). Les choses parlent du quotidien de drames humains d'une dimension historique.

S'affirmer et persévérer

La force artistique des photographies de Martin Rosswog se nourrit avant tout de deux volontés. Il y a d'un côté la «volonté d'esthétique» qui s'affirme contre toutes les résistances, où l'ordonnancement artistique de la quotidienneté représente aussi un combat contre les réalités avilissantes de la pauvreté. C'est en cela que les clichés de Rosswog sont des documents sur la vitalité, la joie et la volonté de s'affirmer. De l'autre, les photos témoignent d'un attachement aux traditions. Même là où les gens auraient les moyens de s'acheter des poêles plus performants, des lits plus confortables ou des salles de bain plus modernes, ils restent attachés au mobilier ancien. Le rythme de ce qui est familier est plus fort que la mélodie séduisante de la modernité industrielle. Le regard photo artistique sur les deux, attitude plutôt passéiste des gens et leur volonté de vivre et de s'affirmer, confère aux photos de Martin Rosswog une artistique personnelle.

Andreas Graf

1 Rückblende – Befragung einer Generation. DuMont Buchverlag, Cologne, 1985; Menschenbilder – Portraitfotografien von Martin Rosswog. DuMont Buchverlag, Cologne, 1989; Asylbilder. DuMont Buchverlag, Cologne, 1996
2 Ländliche Innenräume. Schirmer & Mosel, Munich, 1996
3 Cf. par ex. Bernd und Hilla Becher: Hochöfen. Schirmer & Mosel, Munich, 1990
4 Pour plus de détails sur cette région, se référer à les tableaux
5 Brigitte Schlüter: Interieurs – der Blick hinter die Fassaden. In: Ländliche Innenräume. Schirmer & Mosel, München, 1990
6 August Sander: Menschen des 20. Jahrhunderts. Schirmer & Mosel, Munich, 1980 (réédition)
7 Walker Evans / James Agee: Let us now praise famous men. Houghton Mifflin Company, Boston, 1941
8 Albert Renger-Patzsch: Die Halligen. Préface de Johann Johannsen. Avec le concours de Dr. Karl Häberlin à Wik sur Föhr. Albertus, Berlin, 1927
9 Paul Strand: Un paese. Texte de Cesare Zavattini. Aperture, New York, 1997 (réédition)
10 Paul Strand: Les Hébrides. Texte de François Nourissier. Lausanne, 1962. Édition all.: Paul Strand, Basil Davidson: Land der Gräser. Die Äußeren Hebriden. VEB Kunst, Dresden, o.J.

Reykjavik
Oslo
Stockholm
Helsinki
Tallinn
Moscow
Riga
Copenhagen
Dublin
Vilnius
Minsk
Amsterdam
London
Berlin
Warsaw
Brussels
Kiev
Luxemburg
Paris
Prague
Bratislava
Vienna
Kischinau
Bern
Budapest
Ljubljana
Zagreb
Bucuresti
Sarajevo
Belgrade
Lisbon
Madrid
Sofia
Rome
Istanbul
Tirana
Skopje
Athens
Rabat
Algiers
Tunis

Tafeln | Tableaux | Plates

County Kerry lies in the south-west of the Republic of Ireland and consists largely of three peninsulas which reach out into the Atlantic Ocean. The Gulf Stream guarantees a mild climate. The most northerly of the three peninsulas is Dingle, location of the town of the same name. In the far west is the village of Dunquin (in Irish, Dun Chaoin), close to Slea Head, the most westerly point in Europe. In their everyday lives, the older people still speak Irish (Gaelic). The façades of the houses, like the interiors, are colorfully painted; the dresser, used among other things for displaying china, is the showpiece of the house. There is a small open fireplace, fueled by peat. The Iveragh peninsula includes Ireland's highest mountain range, MacGillycuddy's Reeks; the tallest peak is 1040 meters above sea level. The farmers' main source of income comes from cattle and sheep. Tourism is increasingly becoming an important part of the regional economy.

Ireland | Irland | Irlande

Die Region Kerry liegt im Südwesten der Republik Irland und besteht im Wesentlichen aus drei Halbinseln, die in den Atlantik hineinragen. Der Golfstrom sorgt für ein mildes Klima. Die nördlichste der Halbinseln heißt Dingle, hier liegt auch die gleichnamige Stadt; ganz im Westen befindet sich die Gemeinde Dunquin (gälisch Dun Chaoin) mit Slea Head, dem westlichsten Punkt Europas. Umgangssprache der älteren Menschen ist nach wie vor Gälisch. Die Fassaden der Häuser sowie die Innenräume sind farbenfroh gestrichen, der Geschirrschrank (englisch dresser) mit den offen ausgestellten Tellern wird zum Schmuckstück der Wohnung. Torf dient als Brennstoff für die kleinen offenen Kamine. Auf der Halbinsel Iveragh liegt die höchste Gebirgskette Irlands, die Mac Gillicuddy Reeks (1040 m). Haupterwerb der Landwirte ist die Rinder- und Schafzucht. Der Tourismus entwickelt sich mehr und mehr zu einem wichtigen Wirtschaftszweig dieser Region.

Le comté de Kerry, au sud-ouest de la république d'Irlande, se compose essentiellement de trois grandes péninsules qui s'enfoncent à l'ouest dans l'Atlantique. Il bénéficie d'un climat doux grâce au courant du Gulf Stream. La plus septentrionale de ces trois presqu'îles, la péninsule de Dingle avec la ville du même nom, est occupée à son extrémité ouest par la commune de Dunquin (Dun Chaoin en gaélique), près de laquelle le promontoire de Slea Head marque la pointe la plus occidentale d'Europe. Le gaélique continue d'être parlé couramment par les habitants les plus âgés. Les façades ainsi que les pièces des maisons sont peintes de couleurs vives. Le principal objet de décoration est un grand buffet (anglais dresser), genre de vaisselier rempli d'assiettes. On se chauffe à la tourbe que l'on brûle dans de petites cheminées. La péninsule d'Iveragh est formée par la plus haute chaîne de montagnes d'Irlande: les Mac Gillicuddy Reeks (1040 m). Si l'élevage des bœufs et des moutons constitue la principale activité des paysans, le tourisme, en constant développement, est devenu une importante source de revenus de la région.

Céad Míle
Fáilte

SALT

9

I

3

I.

God's Peace be to this House

chroí ró-
naofa íosa,
is asatsa atá
muinín agam!

POPE JOHN
SAXA
TABLE SALT

2.

2

7

I

owcem
ement
paint

M. F. QUIRKE
& SONS LTD.

Pitching too high for
Rome bums

39

Region: Outer Hebrides

The Outer Hebrides, with their large islands Lewis and Harris in the north and North and South Uist in the south, lie off the Scottish coast in the far Northwest. The stormy climate is the reason for the scarcity of vegetation; the islands are virtually treeless and the soil is poor. As in the days when Scotland was ruled by its nobility, the farmers are tenants, or as they say here, crofters. All that they own are their houses. Cattle and sheep still form the mainstay of the farming economy. Many young people have had to seek work on the mainland or overseas, as there is little employment on the islands apart from salmon farming. It is the old who are left behind.

Scotland | Schottland | Écosse

Region: Western Isles, Äußere Hebriden

Die Äußeren Hebriden mit den größeren Inseln Lewis und Harris im Norden und North- und South Uist im Süden liegen im äußersten Nordwesten vor der Küste Schottlands. Auf Grund der rauen Witterung, der heftigen Stürme ist die Vegetation karg, die Inseln sind nahezu baumlos und die Böden schlecht. Wie zu Zeiten des schottischen Adels bewirtschaften die Bauern überwiegend als Pächter (crofter) ihre Acker- und Weideflächen, lediglich die Wohnhäuser sind in Privatbesitz. Die Landwirte betreiben heute wie früher Rinder- und Schafzucht. Viele junge Menschen müssen sich auf dem Festland oder in Übersee Arbeit suchen, denn Arbeitsplätze in größerer Zahl gibt es auf den Inseln nur auf den Lachs-Farmen. Zurück bleiben die Alten.

Région: Western Isles, Hébrides extérieures

Situées au large de l'extrême nord-ouest de la côte écossaise, les Hébrides extérieures comprennent les grandes îles de Lewis and Harris au nord et le groupe des North et South Uist au sud. Ces îles sont presque entièrement dépourvues d'arbres et les sols, couverts d'une maigre végétation, sont assez pauvres en raison de la rudesse du climat et de la violence des tempêtes. Comme à l'époque de l'aristocratie écossaise, les paysans (crofter) pratiquent l'agriculture et l'élevage sur des terres pour la plupart en fermage; seules les habitations appartiennent à des particuliers. L'élevage de bœufs et de moutons demeure la principale activité agricole. Beaucoup de jeunes insulaires sont aujourd'hui contraints de travailler en Écosse continentale ou de partir outre-mer car seules les fermes d'élevage de saumon offrent des emplois dans les îles. Seuls les habitants plus âgés y restent.

CHANGE
RAIN
FAIR

4

D & F MacNEIL
APRIL 2000
THE BOX

CO-CHOMUNN
N IOCHDAIR LTD
October
Rowenta

SOUVENIR OF LONDON
CO-CHOMUNN

1

3

D & F MacNEIL
APRIL
2000
MODERN

FLORA

APS

6.

Regions: Häme and Saimaa

The Häme region lies in south-central Finland; its chief town is Tampere. The local people built large farmsteads between the numerous lakes of this formerly agrarian region. The older dwelling houses are built in log-cabin style, with large stoves for heating, cooking and baking. The stoves are fueled with birch logs nearly a meter long. Typical of the region are the numerous out-buildings, such as stable, barn and sauna (usually two, one by the house and the other by the nearby lake), and potato-clamp. The people supplement their income by hunting and fishing. The farms are well spaced, often neighbors live five kilometers apart. During the long winters, the lakes freeze over and are used as short-cuts, avoiding the twisting roads. Saimaa lies in the south-east of Finland and borders on the Russian province of West Karelia. Its largest industry is paper production. The inhabitants of the houses documented here are mainly farmers and fisherfolk.

Finland | Finnland | Finlande

Regionen: Häme und Saimaa

Die Region Häme liegt in der südlichen Mitte Finnlands, Hauptstadt ist Tampere. Die Einheimischen erbauten große Bauernhöfe zwischen zahlreichen Seen in dieser ehemals agrarisch geprägten Region. Die älteren Wohnhäuser errichteten sie im Blockhausstil, mit großen Öfen zum Heizen, Kochen und Backen. Befeuert werden die Öfen mit nahezu einen Meter langen Scheiten aus Birkenholz. Typisch sind die zahlreichen Nebengebäude wie Stall, Scheune, Sauna (meistens zwei, eine am Haus und die zweite am nahe gelegenen See) und Miete. Jagen und Fischen dienen den Menschen als Nebenerwerb. Die Höfe liegen weit auseinander, häufig wohnt der Nachbar 5 km entfernt. In den langen Wintern frieren die Seen zu und werden dann als Pisten genutzt, um kurvenreiche Straßen abzukürzen. Saimaa liegt im Südosten Finnlands und grenzt an das russische West-Karelien. Größter Industriezweig ist die Papierherstellung. Die Bewohner der dokumentierten Häuser waren und sind überwiegend Bauern und Fischer.

Régions: Häme et Saimaa

La région de Häme, dont la capitale est Tampere, se situe au centre de la Finlande méridionale. Les autochtones ont construit de grandes fermes entre les innombrables lacs de cette région jadis agricole. Les plus anciennes sont des maisons de bois de style nordique, avec de grands poêles pour chauffer et faire la cuisine, alimentés par des bûches de bouleau de près de un mètre de long. Typiques sont également les nombreuses dépendances telles que étable, grange, saunas (deux en général: l'un près de l'habitation, l'autre au bord du lac proche) et silo. La chasse et la pêche assurent un revenu supplémentaire aux paysans. Il s'agit d'un habitat assez dispersé; 5 km séparent souvent de la ferme voisine. Durant les longs mois d'hiver, les Finlandais peuvent circuler sur la surface gelée des lacs, un moyen d'éviter les routes sinueuses plus longues.
La région de Saimaa, situé à l'est de la Finlande méridionale, marque la frontière avec la Carélie occidentale russe. La principale activité industrielle est la fabrication du papier. Les habitants des maisons photographiées sont pour la plupart des paysans et des pêcheurs.

246

I

1825 1953

ANA ELÄMÄN ERI KÄÄNTEISSÄ
OSUUSPANKKI

alkaa
päättyy

ANTEISSÄ

I

Region: Western Karelia

Western Karelia lies to the north of St Petersburg (formerly Leningrad), between the Gulf of Finland and Lake Ladoga. Its chief town is Vyborg (in Finnish, Viipuri). The region is characterized by small lakes and flat countryside. Western Karelia was part of Finland until 1940, when it was annexed by the Soviet Union, a status confirmed by treaty in 1947. The Finnish population was expelled, and the region settled with people from all parts of the Soviet Union. Formerly Finnish villages fell into decay and no longer exist. Today, Karelia is impoverished. People from St Petersburg have settled there as involuntary subsistence farmers, living in the city in winter on what they have managed to grow on their dacha in the summer. The former state collective farms have now been privatized, but they continue to be inefficient. These photographs document formerly Finnish farmsteads.

Russia | Russland | Russie

Region: West-Karelien

West-Karelien liegt nördlich von St. Petersburg (früher Leningrad), zwischen dem Finnischen Meerbusen und dem Ladoga-See. Hauptstadt ist Vyborg (finnisch Viipuri). Kleine Seen und flaches Land kennzeichnen die Region. Bis 1940 gehörte West-Karelien zu Finnland, 1947 fiel das Gebiet an die Sowjetunion. Die finnische Bevölkerung wurde vertrieben und das Land mit Menschen aus allen Teilen der UdSSR besiedelt. Einst finnische Dörfer verfielen und existieren nicht mehr. Heute ist Karelien ein verarmter Landstrich. Menschen aus St. Petersburg haben sich dort notgedrungen als Selbstversorger angesiedelt; im Winter wohnen sie in der Großstadt und leben dort von dem, was sie im Sommer auf ihrer Datscha angebaut haben. Die ehemals staatlichen landwirtschaftlichen Genossenschaften sind privatisiert, arbeiten aber bisher ineffektiv. Dokumentiert wurden ehemals finnische bäuerliche Anwesen.

Région: Carélie occidentale

La Carélie occidentale, qui a pour capitale Vyborg (finlandais Viipuri), s'étend au nord de Saint-Pétersbourg (ancienne Leningrad), entre le golfe de Finlande et le lac Ladoga. Son paysage plat est parsemé d'innombrables petits lacs. Après avoir appartenu à la Finlande jusqu'en 1940, la Carélie occidentale fut annexée par l'Union soviétique en 1947, qui en expulsa la population finlandaise pour la remplacer par des citoyens originaires de différentes régions de l'U.R.S.S. Bon nombre de villages jadis finlandais sont tombés en ruines et ont fini par disparaître totalement. La Carélie est aujourd'hui une région appauvrie. Des habitants de Saint-Pétersbourg, venus s'y établir contre leur gré, vivent en autarcie; ils passent l'hiver dans la grande ville et se nourrissent des produits potagers de leur datcha. La privatisation des anciennes coopératives agricoles d'État n'a cependant pas rendu ces exploitations plus rentables. Les photographies sont celles de quelques vieilles propriétés rurales finlandaises.

I

I

Tide

3

I

7

9

I

I

3

ПОЛЮС-2

ROCHAS

Region: Memelland

The Memel (or Neman) River today forms the border between the Russian enclave of Kaliningradskaya Oblast and Lithuania. Towards the Baltic coast, the land is flat; the Neman delta is boggy and inaccessible and empties into the Courland Lagoon, separated from the rest of the Baltic Sea by the narrow Courland Spit.
Until the turn of the 20th century, the extensive bogs in the delta were still being drained for farming, and settlements were established. Before the end of the war in 1945, a large part of the population included was German. Of the large German farmsteads, often little remains but the foundations. Depicted in this book are a Lithuanian farm and two houses owned by mixed German-Lithuanian couples.

Lithuania | Litauen | Lituanie

Region: Memelland

Die Memel ist heute Grenzfluss zu der russischen Enklave Kaliningradskaja Oblast. Zur Ostsee hin wird das Land flach, das Memeldelta ist moorig und unzugänglich. Vorgelagert ist die Kurische Nehrung mit dem Kurischen Haff.
Noch bis zur Wende zum 20. Jahrhundert wurden die großen Moore im Delta urbar gemacht und dort Kolonien gegründet. Bis Kriegsende 1945 gab es einen hohen deutschen Bevölkerungsanteil. Von den großen deutschen Bauernhöfen sind heute oft nur noch die Fundamente zu sehen. Im Buch abgebildet sind ein litauisches Anwesen und zwei durch Heirat deutsch-litauische Häuser.

Région: Klaipëda

La région bordant la mer Baltique est une vaste plaine traversée par le fleuve Niémen, qui marque la frontière entre la Lituanie et l'enclave russe de Kaliningradskaya Oblast. Le delta du fleuve, marécageux et inaccessible, est séparé de la mer par la longue bande lagunaire du golfe de Kourski.
Les grands marais du delta furent peu à peu drainés puis peuplés jusqu'au tournant du XXe siècle. Mais, alors qu'une grande partie de la population était allemande jusqu'à la fin de la guerre en 1945, il ne reste plus aujourd'hui que quelques vestiges des grandes fermes allemandes de cette époque, illustrées dans cet ouvrage par une propriété lituanienne et deux habitations lituano-allemandes.

1.

47

GOLLNER

Янтарь

I

3

I

Švarus vanduo.
Kriaukleliai

Švarus vanduo.

Regions: Dolny Śląsk (Lower Silesia), Podhale, Podlasie

The two stone houses in the Gory Sowie or Owl Mountains of Lower Silesia are former German farmsteads, which have been occupied for the last 50 years by Poles expelled from what is now the Ukraine. The stoves are of German manufacture. Once largely agricultural, the region is now wooded. The climate is cold and wet.

The old houses in the Podhale region at the foot of the High Tatra mountains were built by local people in log-cabin style. Typical are the rough-hewn, untreated trunks in the interiors. Here, unlike in northern Poland, the farms were not nationalized, with the result that the farmers of southern Poland have always preserved their independence.

Podlasie borders on Belarus and Lithuania. The old houses here are also built in log-cabin style. Near Białowiéza is Europe's most extensive stretch of primeval forest, with a stock of European bison. The farmers are independent, owning their own land, although the arable areas are very small and still plowed with horses in some cases. This region of Poland is becoming more and more impoverished. While the young are forced to migrate to the towns, only the old remain.

Poland | Polen | Pologne

Regionen: Dolny Śląsk (Niederschlesien), Podhale, Podlasie

Die beiden vorgestellten Steinhäuser im Gory Sowie (Eulengebirge) in Niederschlesien sind ehemalige deutsche Anwesen, die seit über 50 Jahren von aus der heutigen Ukraine vertriebenen Polen bewohnt werden. Die Öfen stammen von deutschen Ofenbauern. Das früher stark landwirtschaftlich genutzte Gebiet ist heute bewaldet, das Klima ist kalt und regnerisch.
Die alten Häuser der Region Podhale am Fuß der Hohen Tatra erbauten die Einheimischen im Blockhausstil. Typisch sind die nur leicht behauenen, unbehandelt gelassenen Stämme im Innenraum. Eine Verstaatlichung der landwirtschaftlichen Höfe wie im Norden Polens fand hier nicht statt, so dass die Bauern Südpolens immer autonom blieben.
Podlasie grenzt an Weißrussland und Litauen. Die alten Häuser sind ebenfalls im Blockhausstil gebaut. Bei Bialowiéza befindet sich der größte Urwald Europas mit Wisentbestand. Die Bauern sind selbstständig mit eigenem Landbesitz, allerdings sind die Ackerflächen sehr klein und werden zum Teil noch mit Pferden bestellt. Dieser Landstrich Polens verarmt heute zunehmend. Die Jugend zieht notgedrungen in die Städte, nur die Alten bleiben.

Régions: Dolny Śląsk (Basse Silésie), Podhale, Podlasie

Ces deux maisons de pierre de la région de Gory Sowie (les Monts tabulaires), en Basse Silésie, sont d'anciennes propriétés allemandes habitées depuis plus d'un demi-siècle par des Polonais expulsés de l'actuelle Ukraine. Les poêles sont également d'origine allemande. Cette région au climat froid et pluvieux, aujourd'hui boisée, a longtemps connu une importante activité agricole.
Les vieilles maisons de la région de Podhale, au pied des Hautes Tatras, présentent les caractéristiques du style local: assemblage de troncs d'arbres non traités, même à l'intérieur. Les paysans du sud de la Pologne ont conservé leur autonomie car les exploitations agricoles n'y ont pas été nationalisées comme dans le nord.
Bordée par la Biélorussie et la Lituanie, la Podlasie abrite près de Bialowiéza la plus grande forêt vierge d'Europe, où existe même une réserve de bisons. Les vieilles maisons sont également en bois. Si les paysans sont propriétaires de leurs terres, les surfaces cultivées sont très petites et souvent labourées encore avec des chevaux. Cette région de la Pologne s'appauvrit aujourd'hui de plus en plus, ce qui oblige les jeunes à émigrer vers les villes. Il ne reste plus que les personnes âgées.

9

I

I

5

7

I

I

LOCK UP
True Story
BRUCE LEE
unbesiegt bis in den Tod

1

Regions: Zakarpatskaya (Transcarpathia) and Ukrayinski Karpaty (Western Carpathia)

In the south, Transcarpathia borders on the Great Hungarian plain. The region's capital is Uzhgorod. The warm summers allow wine, fruit and vegetables to flourish both on the plain and on the southern slopes of the Carpathian mountains. Until 1920, the region was part of Austria, but was then divided between Czechoslovakia and Hungary. In 1945 it was annexed by the Soviet Union, and since the break-up of the USSR it has become part of the Ukraine. Near the Hungarian border there are many Hungarian villages, in which Hungarian is spoken exclusively. In the formerly German-speaking villages, Hungarians and Slovaks now live alongside the still numerous ethnic Germans.
The Western Carpathian region is mountainous and heavily wooded. The steep slopes cannot be cultivated by tractor, the meadows are still mown with scythes and sickles. The farmers' produce is just about sufficient for their own requirements. Alongside agriculture, forestry is an important part of the local economy. The houses, like those in eastern Poland and in the Romanian part of Carpathia, are built in log-cabin style. Large stoves with a sleeping recess help to survive the cold winters.

Ukraine | Ukraine | Ukraine

Regionen: Transkarpatien und Ukrajinski Karpaty (West-Karpaten)

Transkarpatien grenzt im Süden an die Donau-Theiß-Ebene (Alföld). Die Hauptstadt ist Uschgorod. Die warmen Sommer lassen an den Südhängen der Karpaten und in der Ebene Wein, Obst und Gemüse gedeihen. Bis 1920 gehörte Transkarpatien zu Österreich, fiel dann an die Tschechoslowakei und an Ungarn, 1945 an die UdSSR und ist seit Auflösung der Sowjetunion ukrainisch. Nahe der ungarischen Grenze gibt es viele ungarische Dörfer, in denen ausschließlich Ungarisch gesprochen wird. In ehemals deutschen Dörfern (Barthaus) leben neben den Ungarn und Slowaken noch heute zahlreiche Deutsche.

Die Ukrainischen Karpaten sind sehr gebirgig und waldreich. Die steilen Hänge können nicht mit Traktoren bewirtschaftet werden, die Wiesen werden noch mit Sense und Sichel gemäht. Das Erwirtschaftete der Kleinbauern reicht gerade für den eigenen Bedarf. Neben der Landwirtschaft wird im großen Stil Holzeinschlag betrieben. Die Häuser sind wie in Ostpolen und im rumänischen Teil der Karpaten im Blockhausstil errichtet. Große Öfen mit einer Schlafgelegenheit darauf helfen, die kalten Winter zu überstehen.

Régions: Transcarpatie et Carpates occidentales (Ukrajinski Karpaty)

La Transcarpatie, dont la capitale est Oujgorod, borde au sud la plaine du Danube-Tisza (Alföld). Le climat chaud en été favorise l'agriculture (vigne, fruits et légumes) sur les versants méridionaux des Carpates. Autrichienne jusqu'en 1920, la Transcarpatie passa successivement sous la tutelle de la Tchécoslovaquie et de la Hongrie, puis de l'U.R.S.S. en 1945. Elle appartient à l'Ukraine depuis la dissolution de l'U.R.S.S. Les habitants des villages hongrois proches de la frontière hongroise parlent uniquement le hongrois, tandis que les anciennes bourgades allemandes (comme Barbowo/Barthaus) sont aujourd'hui encore peuplées de nombreux Allemands, en plus des Hongrois et des Slovaques.

Les pentes escarpées des Carpates occidentales, très montagneuses et couvertes de forêts, rendent impossible toute mécanisation de l'agriculture et les prairies sont encore fauchées à la main. Le revenu des petits propriétaires suffit tout juste à satisfaire leurs propres besoins. En plus de l'activité agricole, l'exploitation du bois compte pour une grande part dans l'économie de la région. Les maisons, édifiées en bois, rappellent celles de l'est de la Pologne et des Carpates roumaines. De grands poêles, sur lesquels est installée la literie, aident à mieux supporter les rigueurs de l'hiver.

19.

95

Das letzte Abendmahl

САХАР
ГЕРКУЛЕС
РИС
МУКА
КРУПА
МАННА

PILSNER

95

7

09

I

2

Egyetértés
szeretet vezéreljen
tégedet !

7

2

I

Regions: Maramureş and Kalotaszeg

The Maramureş region in the north of Romania is dominated by the Carpathian mountains. Like on the Ukrainian side, there are high mountain pastures, and purely Ukrainian villages where almost only Russian is spoken. Alongside the peasant economy – collectivization did not take place in this part of Romania – forestry is a major source of income. The first Germans to cross the River Tisza and settle in these valleys were mainly lumberjacks and raftsmen. The style of the farmhouses resembles the Ukrainian style. The rooms are decorated by cloths and hand-knotted carpets. The region is well-known for its wood-carving (seen on gateways, banisters, beams etc.)
The villages in north-western Romania (Kalotaszeg) are inhabited largely by ethnic Hungarians. Their origin enables many to work in affluent Hungary. Here, in foreign lands, the Hungarian traditions of house decoration, costumes and customs have been preserved in a purer form than in Hungary itself.

Romania | Rumänien | Roumanie

Regionen: Maramureş und Kalotaszeg

Die Region Maramureş ganz im Norden Rumäniens wird beherrscht von den gebirgigen Karpaten. Es gibt Hochalmen wie auf ukrainischer Seite und rein ukrainische Dörfer, in denen fast ausschließlich Russisch gesprochen wird. Neben der kleinbäuerlichen Landwirtschaft – in diesem Teil Rumäniens wurde nicht kollektiviert – ist die Forstwirtschaft ein wichtiger Erwerbszweig. Die ersten Deutschen, die über die Theiß kommend in den Tälern siedelten, waren überwiegend Holzfäller und Flößer. Der Baustil der Bauernhäuser gleicht dem der ukrainischen. Tücher und selbstgeknüpfte Teppiche dekorieren die Zimmer. Die Region ist bekannt für ihre Holzschnitzkunst (verzierte Toreinfahrten, Geländer, Balken etc.).
Die Dörfer im Nordwesten Rumäniens (Kalotaszeg) werden hauptsächlich von Ungarn bewohnt. Auf Grund ihrer Herkunft haben viele die Möglichkeit, im wohlhabenden Ungarn zu arbeiten. Hier in der Fremde haben sich ungarische Traditionen im Dekor der Wohnungen, in Trachten, Sitten und Gebräuchen reiner erhalten als in Ungarn selbst.

Régions: Maramureş et Kalotaszeg

La province de Maramureş, à l'extrême nord de la Roumanie, est dominée par la chaîne des Carpates. Les hauts alpages sont parsemés de fermes, comme du côté ukrainien, et de villages purement ukrainiens dont les habitants parlent presque exclusivement russe. L'exploitation du bois et l'agriculture, pratiquée dans de petites exploitations – cette partie de la Roumanie a échappé à la collectivisation – sont les deux principales activités de la région. Les premiers Allemands qui, venus par la Tisza, s'installèrent dans les vallées, étaient pour la plupart des bûcherons et des Flotteurs. Le style des habitations rurales, décorées d'étoffes et de tapis tissés à la main, rappelle celui des fermes d'Ukraine. La région est célèbre pour son artisanat sur bois (portes cochères, rampes, poutres sculptées, etc.).
Les villages du nord-ouest de la Roumanie (Kalotaszeg) sont surtout habités par des Hongrois, que leur origine autorise à travailler en Hongrie voisine, économiquement plus riche. La tradition hongroise perpétuée ici – dans la décoration des habitations, les costumes régionaux, les us et coutumes – est encore plus authentique qu'en Hongrie elle-même.

31

1999

1999

CALENDAR CRESTIN ORTODOX
Opinia
1996

2000
O actiune barbara, de tip terorist
PDSR!
PDSR!
PDSR!

I

3

Region: Alföd (Great Hungarian Plain)

The houses depicted are in villages on the left bank of the Danube, near the town of Kalocsa. Harta was formerly inhabited by ethnic Germans. The village looks as if it had come straight off the drawing-board, with parallel streets lined by neatly parceled farms. The living-quarters face the street, with the animal sheds and gardens to the rear. The people formerly earned their livelihood from agriculture, Danube navigation, and crafts, in particular joinery. These days, items of elaborately painted Harta furniture are now regarded as antique rarities. The crops grown on the flat fields include corn (maize) and paprika. Under the communists, agriculture was collectivized, and each farmer retained only a small piece of land for his own subsistence. The old clay-brick houses contain large stoves, as the winters can be very harsh.

Hungary | Ungarn | Hongrie

Region: Alföld (Donau-Theiß-Tiefland)

Die abgebildeten Wohnungen sind in Dörfern am linken Donau-Ufer aufgenommen, nahe der Stadt Kalocsa. Harta (Hartau) ist eine ehemalige deutsche Ansiedlung. Das Dorf wirkt wie am Reißbrett entworfen, die Straßen verlaufen parallel zueinander, die Hofparzellen liegen aufgereiht nebeneinander.
Zur Straße hin liegen die Wohnräume, nach hinten Stallungen und Garten. Erwerbszweige waren früher Landwirtschaft, Donauschifffahrt und Handwerk, besonders das Möbelhandwerk. Hartauer Möbel mit ihren kunstvollen Bemalungen gelten heute als antike Rarität. Auf den flachen Feldern werden u.a. Paprika und Mais angebaut. Der Kommunismus brachte die Kollektivierung der Landwirtschaft, den Bauern verblieb nur ein kleines Stück Land zur Selbstversorgung. In den Häusern, die früher aus Lehmziegeln gebaut wurden, stehen große Öfen, da die Winter sehr streng sein können.

Région: Alföld (plaine du Danube et de la Tisza)

Les maisons photographiées appartiennent à des villages de la rive gauche du Danube, à proximité de la ville de Kalocsa. Celui de Harta, une ancienne colonie allemande (Hartau), présente un plan rigoureux de rues parallèles, le long desquelles s'alignent les fermes. Les pièces d'habitation donnent sur la rue; étables et jardin occupent la partie arrière. Les principales activités de cette région de plaine étaient autrefois l'agriculture, la batellerie sur le Danube et l'artisanat, notamment la fabrication de mobilier. Les meubles peints de Harta sont aujourd'hui recherchés comme des pièces d'antiquité rares. Dans les champs plats, on cultive entre autres du poivron rouge et du maïs. Le collectivisme n'a laissé aux paysans qu'un lopin de terre pour assurer leur autosubsistance. Les fermes, autrefois construites en briques d'argile, disposent de grands poêles pour les très rudes hivers.

ORION

21
Salgó

Minden jóakaratú embernek
GT 23

SOKOL-403

19
99

Weißer
Riese
FINOMLISZ

ANNO 1991
ANNO 1991

A rend és tisztaság

Region: Oberbergisches Land

The selection of pictures is restricted to the village of Remshagen in the Oberbergisches Land. This region lies some 40 kilometers to the east of the Rhineland conurbations of Cologne and Düsseldorf. Agricultural activity is centered more and more on just a few farms, which – as a result of the climate – concentrate on beef and dairy production. Until the 1950s there was a flourishing quarrying industry in the region and for many, the quarries near Remshagen provided a useful second job. Typical of the Oberbergisches Land are the half-timbered houses with slate-covered walls to the west, facing the prevailing wind.

Germany | Deutschland | Allemagne

Region: Oberbergisches Land

Die Auswahl der Bilder beschränkt sich auf den Ort Remshagen im Oberbergischen Land. Das Oberbergische Land liegt ca. 40 km östlich der Ballungsgebiete um die Großstädte Köln und Düsseldorf. Die Landwirtschaft konzentriert sich mehr und mehr auf wenige Bauernhöfe, die klimabedingt überwiegend Rinderzucht und Milchwirtschaft betreiben. Noch bis in die 1950er Jahre hinein dominierte die Steinindustrie (Grauwacke). Für viele boten die Steinbrüche rund um Remshagen einen Nebenerwerb. Typisch für das Oberbergische Land sind die Fachwerkhäuser mit der verschieferten Westseite (Wetterseite).

Région: Oberberg

Les photographies sélectionnées ne concernent que la localité de Remshagen, dans l'Oberberg. L'activité agricole de cette région, située à près de 40 km à l'est des conurbations autour des grandes villes de Cologne et de Düsseldorf, se concentre de plus en plus, pour des raisons climatiques, dans quelques fermes d'élevage bovin (viande et lait). L'exploitation de la pierre (grès des houillères) a occupé une place prépondérante dans l'économie jusque dans les années 1950. Les carrières autour de Remshagen assuraient un gagne-pain supplémentaire aux habitants. Les colombages et la couverture d'ardoises de la façade ouest des maisons (côté du toit exposé aux intempéries) sont caractéristiques du style de l'Oberberg.

BOSCH

SABA
BLAUPUNKT

SUZUKI
GM·LJ 62

VILLINGEN
jeden Garten.

3

MEDION
SANWA 7040

Regions: Pays de la Loire, Creuse, Périgord

The Pays de la Loire region lies in France's mid-west, and is characterized by the many branches of the Loire river. There are two large towns, Nantes and Angers. The mild climate and the large fields make this a high-yield farming region. The farms, therefore, are large and prosperous.
The Creuse region has always been seen as France's poorhouse. The terrain is mountainous and heavily wooded, and the small, poor farmhouses are mostly abandoned these days. Farming in this region has become uneconomic. The stone houses used to be heated with open fires fueled by wood.
Périgord is the region around the town of Périgueux in the southwest of France. The warm climate makes it possible to grow wine, fruit and vegetables.

France | Frankreich | France

Regionen: Pays de la Loire, Creuse, Périgord

Die Region Pays de la Loire liegt im mittleren Westen Frankreichs und wird geprägt durch den weit verzweigten Flusslauf der Loire. Größere Städte sind Nantes und Angers. Das milde Klima und die großflächigen Felder ermöglichen eine ertragreiche Landwirtschaft. Die Höfe sind entsprechend groß und wohlhabend.
Die Region Creuse galt seit jeher als das Armenhaus Frankreichs. Die Gegend ist gebirgig und waldreich, die kleinen und ärmlichen Bauernhöfe sind heute meist verlassen. Landwirtschaft in dieser Region ist unrentabel geworden. In den Steinhäusern wurde früher mit offenen Kaminen geheizt, Brennstoff war Holz.
Périgord nennt sich die Region um die Stadt Périgueux im Südwesten Frankreichs. Das warme Klima ermöglicht Wein-, Obst- und Gemüseanbau.

Régions: Pays de la Loire, Creuse, Périgord

Le paysage de la région des Pays de la Loire, dans le centre-ouest de la France, est marqué par le cours de la Loire et de ses nombreux affluents. Nantes et Angers sont les villes les plus importantes. La douceur du climat et la grandeur des parcelles cultivées expliquent la richesse de l'agriculture, assurée par de grandes exploitations prospères.
La Creuse, couverte de plateaux montagneux et de forêts, a toujours été considérée comme la région la plus déshéritée de la France. Les petites fermes sont aujourd'hui pour la plupart abandonnées car l'agriculture n'est plus rentable. Le chauffage des maisons en pierre était jadis assuré par des cheminées dans lesquelles on faisait brûler du bois.
Le Périgord, une région du sud-ouest de la France autour de la ville de Périgueux, bénéficie d'un climat doux favorable aux cultures fruitières et maraîchères, ainsi qu'à la vigne.

QUAKER OATS
Flocons d'Avoine
SUCRE
FARINE
CAFE
THÉ
EPICES

Café

1992
BANQUE POPULAIRE
DU CENTRE
vins
Carrousel

Biscottes Jacquet

PHILIPS

SINGER

SINGER

OMO

San Martín de la Vega del Alberche, Castilia Vieja

House 1; Haus 1; Maison n°1 (1996)	
Kitchen-cum-living-room; Wohnküche; Chambre-cuisine	353, 354, 355
Hall; Flur; Vestibule	357
House 2; Haus 2; Maison n°2 (1996)	
Interior courtyard and front door; Innenhof und Hauseingang; Cour et entrée de la maison	358, 359
Kitchen-cum-living-room; Wohnküche; Chambre-cuisine	361
Hall; Flur; Vestibule	362, 363
Bedroom; Schlafzimmer; Chambre à coucher	364, 365
View of village; Dorfansicht; Vue du village	366, 367
House 3; Haus 3; Maison n°3 (1999)	
Kitchen-cum-living-room; Wohnküche; Chambre-cuisine	369, 370, 371
Hall; Flur; Vestibule	373
House 4; Haus 4; Maison n°4 (1999)	
Gateway and house; Toreinfahrt und Wohnhaus; Porte cochère et maison d'habitation	374, 375
Hall; Flur; Vestibule	377
Kitchen; Küche; Cuisine	378, 379
Living room; Wohnzimmer; Salle de séjour	381

Region: Castilia Vieja

The village of San Martín de la Vega del Alberche lies on a plateau some 1500 meters above sea level to the north of the Gredos, a mountain range with peaks of up to 2700 meters. The nearest large town is Avila. The summers are very hot and dry, while the winters are cold with a lot of snow. The village is compact; there are no outlying farms or houses. The inhabitants are mostly elderly people who have not yet given up farming (cattle and horsebreeding). The young migrate to the larger towns and cities. Almost all of the stone houses have enclosed interior courtyards, around which are grouped the relatively dark living-quarters with their small windows.

Spain | Spanien | Espagne

Region: Alt-Kastilien

Das Dorf San Martín de la Vega del Alberche liegt auf einem Hochplateau ca. 1500 m über NN nördlich der Gredos, einer Gebirgskette mit Gipfeln bis zu 2700 m. Die nächstgrößte Stadt ist Avila. Die Sommer sind sehr heiß und trocken, die Winter kalt und schneereich. Das Dorf weist ein in sich geschlossenes Bild auf, es gibt keine Höfe oder Häuser außerhalb der Ansiedlung. Bei den Bewohnern handelt es sich meist um ältere Menschen, die die Landwirtschaft (Rinder- und Pferdezucht) noch nicht aufgegeben haben. Die Jugend wandert ab in die großen Städte. Fast alle der aus Stein gebauten Häuser haben ummauerte Innenhöfe, um die herum sich relativ dunkle Wohnräume mit nur kleinen Fensteröffnungen gruppieren.

Région: Castille

Le village de San Martín de la Vega del Alberche perche sur un haut plateau d'environ 1500 m d'altitude, au nord de la sierra de Gredos, une chaîne de montages qui culmine à 2700 m. La plus grande ville voisine est Avila. Les étés sont très chauds et secs, les hivers froids et enneigés. Le village semble replié sur lui-même; il n'y a ni fermes ni aucune autre forme d'habitat alentour. La population se compose surtout de personnes âgées qui n'ont pas encore renoncé à leur activité agricole (élevage de boeufs et de chevaux). Les jeunes émigrent vers les grandes villes. Presque toutes les maisons en pierre sont construites autour d'un patio, sur lequel s'ouvrent des pièces relativement sombres, percées uniquement de petites fenêtres.

ABRIL 1996

1993

«TININ»
ANGELINES
GRUNDIG

Callos a la madrileña
Electrodomésticos AVENIDA
T.V. - VIDEO - HI-FI
DISTRIBUIDOR DE Corberó PARA AVILA Y PROVINCIA
S.A.T. - MUEBLES DE COCINA
Avda. José Antonio, 22 AVILA Tel. 920 22 06 61 - Fax 920 22 01 62
1999
Marzo
1 2 3 4 5 6 7
8 9 10 11 12 13 14
15 16 17 18 19 20 21
22 23 24 25 26 27 28
29 30 31
Abril
1 2 3 4
5 6 7 8 9 10 11
12 13 14 15 16 17 18
19 20 21 22 23 24 25
26 27 28 29 30
VISCOUNT

AYUNTAMIENTO

14

ASEPEYO

GLOBS
Cola
99

Acknowledgments

I should like to thank the many people who have supported my work in the various countries of Europe. It was their commitment which gained me entry to many houses in the first place.
My particular thanks are due to Birgit and Wilfried Kunze; Maureen Curran and Micheál Delany (Ireland); Anna Mackinnon and Neil MacMillan (Western Isles, Scotland); Clemens-Peter Haase of the Goethe Institute; Raimo Lietsala, Osmo Koskinen and Sirkku Kuisma (Finland); Timofeeva Tamara (Karelia); Ulla Lachauer for her support of my work in Lithuania; Teodor Iganowicz and Renata Chudoba (Poland); Oksana Simomrija, Wolodija Olenitsch and Prof. Georg Melika (Transcarpathia, Ukraine); Dr Konrad Gündisch of the Federal Institute for Eastern German Culture and History in Oldenburg, whose thorough knowledge and numerous contacts made my work in Romania possible; Dr Klára K. Csilléry, Imre Romschitsch and Thomas Schill (Hungary); Dr Jan Carstensen and Dr Josef Mangold (Germany) – both of them students of folk culture, they made decisive contributions to the project and gave me many valuable hints; Rosine Gaspard and Astrid Guesnet (France); and the Gutiérrez-Martin family from San Martín de la Vega del Alberche (Spain).
It goes without saying that my thanks are due above all to all those who allowed me to photograph the insides of their houses. I have fond memories of our meetings.

Martin Rosswog, Kurtenbach, June 2000

Dank

Ich möchte den vielen Personen danken, die meine fotografische Arbeit in den verschiedenen europäischen Ländern unterstützten. Durch ihr Engagement wurde der Zutritt zu vielen Wohnungen erst möglich.
Ein besonderer Dank geht an Birgit und Wilfried Kunze; Maureen Curran und Michéal Delany (Irland); Anna Mackinnon und Neil MacMillan (Western Isles, Schottland); Clemens-Peter Haase vom Goethe-Institut, Raimo Lietsala, Osmo Koskinen und Sirkku Kuisma (Finnland); Timofeeva Tamara (Russisch-Karelien); Ulla Lachauer für die Unterstützung meiner Arbeit in Litauen; Teodor Iganowicz und Renata Chudoba (Polen); Oksana Simomrija, Wolodija Olenitsch und Prof. Dr. Georg Melika (Transkarpatien, Ukraine); Dr. Konrad Gündisch vom Bundesinstitut für ostdeutsche Kultur und Geschichte in Oldenburg, der mir dank seiner fundierten Kenntnisse und zahlreichen Kontakte die Arbeit in Rumänien ermöglichte; Dr. Klára K. Csilléry, Imre Romschitsch und Thomas Schill (Ungarn); Dr. Jan Carstensen und Dr. Josef Mangold (Deutschland), beide Volkskundler, sie förderten maßgebend das Projekt und gaben mir wertvolle Hinweise; Rosine Gaspard und Astrid Guesnet (Frankreich) und die spanische Familie Gutiérrez-Martin aus San Martín de la Vega del Alberche.
Selbstverständlich gilt mein Dank vor allem den Menschen, die mir das Ablichten ihrer Wohnräume gestatteten. Ich erinnere mich gerne an diese Begegnungen.

Martin Rosswog, Kurtenbach, Juni 2000

Remerciements

Je tiens à remercier les nombreuses personnes ayant eu l'amabilité de soutenir mon travail photographique dans les divers pays d'Europe. Sans leur engagement, beaucoup de portes d'habitations me seraient restées closes.
Je tiens tout particulièrement à remercier Birgit et Wilfried Kunze, Maureen Curran et Michéal Delany (Irlande); Anna Mackinnon et Neil MacMillan (Iles Hébrides, Écosse); Clemens-Peter Haase du Goethe-Institut, Raimo Lietsala, Osmo Koskinen et Sirkku Kuisma (Finlande); Timofeeva Tamara (Carélie russe); Ulla Lachauer pour le soutient de mon travail en Lituanie; Teodor Iganowicz et Renata Chudoba (Pologne); Oksana Simomrija, Wolodija Olenitsch et Prof. Dr. Georg Melika (Transcarpatie, Ukraine); Dr. Konrad Gündisch du Bundesinstitut für ostdeutsche Kultur und Geschichte d'Oldenbourg qui, grâce à ses connaissances fondées et ses innombrables contacts m'a rendu possible mon travail en Roumanie; Dr. Klára K. Csilléry, Imre Romschitsch et Thomas Schill (Hongrie); Dr. Jan Cartensen et Dr. Josef Mangold (Allemagne), tous deux folkloristes, ils encouragèrent le projet de manière déterminante et me donnèrent de précieuses indications; Rosine Gaspard et Astrid Guesnet (France) et enfin, la famille espagnole Gutiérrez-Martin de San Martín de la Vega del Alberche.
Mes remerciements vont bien sûr avant tout à toutes les personnes qui m'autorisèrent à photographier leurs intérieurs. Je me souviens avec plaisir de ces rencontres.

Martin Rosswog, Kurtenbach, juin 2000